SOCIAL MARKETING SUPERSTARS

In Praise of
SOCIAL MARKETING SUPERSTARS

You will long feel gratitude to Cydney O'Sullivan for putting these secrets all together for you between the covers of a book, the easy way to learn them. If I were you, I wouldn't wait too long to apply them.

—**Jay Conrad Levinson,** The Father of Guerrilla Marketing
Author, "Guerrilla Marketing" series of books
The best known marketing brand in history
Named one of the 100 best business books ever written
Over 21 million sold; now in 62 languages

"I love this book... and for me to say that is rare — especially publicly like this (I only give endorsements if and when I find something that is exceptionally rare). Why do I love it? Simply this: I find that as I'm reading through these pages the ideas are springing to mind — so many in fact that it's hard to concentrate on reading the next part! And for me, that's the sign of a great book. A resource that rewards you every time you pick it up..."

—**Brett McFall**, www.brettmcfall.com, Author and Internet Marketer

Cydney O'Sullivan has nailed it with her new book *Social Marketing Superstars*. I couldn't put it down and can't recommend it highly enough. Full of insightful, yet practical gems to fire up your web success. I only wish something like this was around when I was getting started!

—**Sari Mustonen-Kirk**, Author & Founder www.uROk.tv
Global podcast audience of 1.5 million+

The Web offers hundreds of booksellers selling thousands of titles on how to be a success in your own business, promising you can make millions. *Social Marketing Superstars* is in a class by itself-offering detailed, real-world advice from people who are not only uncommonly successful but willing to share the keys to how they did it, and how you can do it, too. There is nothing better than learning the "how-to's" from men and women whose self-made millions are the best evidence of their business wisdom.

—**William L. Simon**, New York Times and International Bestselling Author

If you know your business should be on the internet, let alone social media's like Facebook, LinkedIn and Google+, and know that the longer you put if off the harder it will be to stand out and succeed in your industry… this book is exactly what you need! My friend Cydney has interviewed 30 extraordinary marketers and asked them the tough questions to help businesses in every industry make money with social marketing. This book is a must have for every manager in business today.

—**Chris Gray**, CEO of Your Empire, Host of 'Your Money Your Call' on Sky News Business Channel and Real Estate Expert on Channel Ten's 'The Renovators'

The world has changed. Companies that have been around are disappearing. New companies are emerging in whole new markets. Social Media has not only changed the field it is defining the field for today and for the future. Cydney has brought together a star list of internet marketers to bring their wisdom, their expertise and direct advice on how to be wildly successful online. If you apply information from just one of these chapters you are ahead of the curve. You apply five or more get ready for dramatic result in your business and brace for yourself for an incredible future.

—**Clinton Swaine**, CEO and Founder of Frontier Trainings, the world leader in experiential business games. www.FrontierTrainings.com

Stuck on how to maximize social media for your business? Then don't wait a minute longer! Read this book as Cydney O'Sullivan interviews 30 of the hottest marketers on the planet who answer the tough questions and give proven ways to leverage these new technologies and strategies for ANY business!

—**Julie Mason**, www.TheSocialMediaPrincess.com

Whether creating a personal brand or a company brand, building social proof or generating targeted traffic social media is now more important than ever. Keeping up with this rapidly changing world is a challenge for anyone, hence the importance of this book. By combining the experience and knowledge of a range of experts this book condenses what works in a manageable, practical and priceless guide. If you want to not only survive but thrive in today's social environment this is a must read.

—**Leon Jay**, Author and CEO FusionHQ Inc, www.FusionHQ.com

In these fast moving times it is critical that entrepreneurs and business leaders constantly explore new ways to connect to their clients and their audience. *Social Marketing Superstars* gives you the step-by-step success strategies of top marketers who are committed to serving and expanding their clients and customers. If you want to reach larger and larger audiences and increase your bottom line follow this Step-By-Step Guide to Social Marketing and watch your business soar.

—**Ardice Farrow**, Best Selling Author & Speaker, www.ArdiceFarrow.com

There's nothing better than reading a book packed with lots of fantastic information and timely wisdom from world class experts—one's who've actually done it. Cydney O'Sullivan has written a must-read book that will advance your social learnings and if you want to create a more successful business than you need to read *Social Marketing Superstars!*

—**Angelique Milojevic**, Author and Main Mastermind, www.BusinessMasterminds.com.au

Cydney has produced a truly remarkable book. Its power lies in the cumulated knowledge of her contributors. Sharing being the hallmark of the social networking phenomenon, here are 30 successful people who are willing to share their stories and wisdom in a way that makes it easy for the reader to apply them to their own business and relationships. If you have talent and vision, but not a lot of money to promote your product and ideas, *Social Marketing Superstars* is filled with innovative and inspiring social marketing strategies... knowledge that will catapult your business and your life to new heights.

—**Judy Winestone**, Learning Consultant, Toronto, Canada

Cydney O'Sullivan is one of the most prolific learners I know. So it's no surprise to me that she's now published her own book—and what a great book it is. It's jam-packed with literally hundreds of useful tips from dozens of experts, to help you explode your financial results through social media. Well done Cydney for putting together such a great 'how to' manual."

—**Dale Beaumont**, Managing Director of Business Blueprint
and Author of 16 Best-Selling Books

With close to a billion people on Facebook, and Google Plus already over 100 million users, Social Media is a major marketing channel for serious online marketers. Cydney O'Sullivan has interviewed a range of business owners who are successfully using social media to grow their business. From multi-millionaires to cutting edge resource providers who are creating tools to make social marketing fast, fun and easy, Cydney has gathered insights that will make a difference to the bottom-line of any business. Cydney's book *Social Marketing Superstars,* and her Millionaires Academy training program show you how to adapt your business to the new rules of "world of mouth marketing"!

—**Dr Daryl Grant**, www.OurInternetSecrets.com

Studies show that more women than men use social media to do what they do best…connect, network and collaborate. If you're a woman with a message that you want the world to hear, with a business you want to grow or a movement you want to launch, social media is THE ticket to getting you there. In her book "Social Marketing Superstars", Cydney O'Sullivan meets you wherever you are on your journey, bringing you an invaluable roadmap for learning and leveraging social marketing so you can do what you came here to do…deliver value, make a difference and make your passion profitable! Don't wait another minute…go get "Social Marketing Superstars" today!

—**Liora Mendeloff**, President & Founder, Women Speakers Association,
WSALive.comEmpowering the voice of women
in 88 countries on 6 of the 7 continents

SOCIAL MARKETING SUPERSTARS

Social Media Mystery To Mastery in 30 Days

CYDNEY O'SULLIVAN

NEW YORK

Social Marketing Superstars
Social Media Mystery to Mastery in 30 Days
A Step-By-Step Success Guide

For general information on our other products and services, please find our contact information online at www.MillionairesAcademy.com

To purchase customized or bulk copies of this book, please visit us online at www.MillionairesAcademy.com/bulk

Image of President Obama is used with permission from The Hunger Project, www.thp.org

Interview with Kim Castle, © Castle Montone, Limited. All Rights Reserved.

ISBN 978-1-61448-217-8 PB
ISBN 978-1-61448-218-5 EB
Library of Congress Control Number: 2012931064

MORGAN JAMES PUBLISHING
The Entrepreneurial Publisher
5 Penn Plaza, 23rd Floor, New York City, New York 10001
(212) 655-5470 office • (516) 908-4496 fax
www.MorganJamesPublishing.com

Cover Design by:
Rachel Lopez
www.r2cdesign.com

Interior Design by:
Bonnie Bushman
bonnie@caboodlegraphics.com

In an effort to support local communities, raise awareness and funds, Morgan James Publishing donates a percentage of all book sales for the life of each book to Habitat for Humanity Peninsula and Greater Williamsburg.
Get involved today, visit
www.MorganJamesBuilds.com.

To my friends and mentors who took the time to share their secrets… and to you; the Curious, Adventurous Entrepreneur willing to explore the new frontiers

CONTENTS

SECTION TWO: BUILD   63

SECTION THREE: CONNECT   119

FOREWORD

Jay Conrad Levinson

Marketing is much more complex and time-consuming now than it used to be. That's how losers see it.

Marketing is much simpler and more exciting now than it used to be. That's how marketing guerrillas see it.

They see three world-changing opportunities that weren't around when marketing came upon this planet.

1. TELEVISION
2. INTERNET
3. SOCIAL MEDIA

At first, as with fire, people misused those opportunities as they learned to use them. The first TV commercials were far sillier than they were motivating. TV was abused long before bright people came around and showed how it can best be used.

Same thing happened with the internet. It didn't come with operating instructions, so many a brave pioneer got lost in cyberspace. The collapse of the internet bubble was easy to see coming. Yet, countless otherwise smart people lost depressing sums of money abusing an opportunity they had yet learned to use.

Can you see what I'm getting at here? Can you see why Cydney O'Sullivan put this breakthrough book together?

The social media is bigger, more important and far more influential than any television channel or internet website. Because of that, it is being abused by misuse every minute of every day.

But here comes the good Ms O'Sullivan proving that it need not be that way. Used properly, social media can make a fortune for you far more rapidly than TV or email. It need not explode in your face before it causes a profit explosion in your bank account.

How do you learn the secrets to detonating that explosion? You talk to the real experts – not the teachers or the writers – but the actual people who can tell you mind-numbing stories of how they did it, how they earned impressive sums of money simply by acting on the secrets of acquiring wealth by knowing their way around the social media.

Those secrets are in this book. Those secrets are clearly revealed by the people who learned them, often, the hard way. You will long feel gratitude to Cydney O'Sullivan for putting them all together for you between the covers of a book, the easy way to learn them.

If I were you, I wouldn't wait too long to apply them.

Lucky you!

Jay Conrad Levinson
DeBary, Florida

Jay Conrad Levinson
The Father of Guerrilla Marketing
Author, "Guerrilla Marketing" series of books
The best known marketing brand in history
Named one of the 100 best business books ever written
Over 21 million sold; now in 62 languages

PREFACE

DC Cordova

Have you ever wanted the ability to look into the future and predict the next big thing that could take your business to a whole other level? In my organization, we are students of R. Buckminster Fuller, a great visionary known as "the Leonardo da Vinci of the 20th century" and one of *Time Magazine*'s top 100 people of that period. So we have been trained to think as Futurists. Once you learn the patterns of thinking that great masters, great visionaries and people with natural ability to predict the future have, one can see what trends may be just around the corner.

I had a glimpse of what is now known as "social media" in the late '90s. I started dreaming of an "Excellerated Portal" where the graduates of our programs, the promoters and supporters of our work, the Masters of our field, associates, close friends and beloveds could be connected – and have a system exciting enough that they would want to join up and stay in communication. I found an expert in creating networks that could possibly achieve that vision. I spent tens of thousands of dollars in development; but it was costly, complicated, and then I'd have to promote it and get all of our graduates and all those other "peeps" to join in. It dragged on for years… so I got busy expanding the business through traditional avenues where I knew with certainty I could succeed… and then a "miracle" occurred: social media was born.

I didn't know that so many others had the same vision…or that this system would one day be available for free, a tool I didn't even have to finance. That would connect us to graduates from all of our programs, all the way back to 1978, our first Business School for Entrepreneurs of its kind; that we would have the ability to find so many of them and connect with thousands more. With well over 80,000 graduates of our trainings, for me social media was a dream come true, as it is for many people all over the world today.

When wondrous new things are created (or found), there is a natural temptation to resist change. I recommend you not resist this change. Some people do care to know what you are doing on a daily or weekly basis, or to read/hear about what you know, or follow up with some fascinating article that you found. It's the most brilliant way to connect with your community.

With this book, finally, someone has asked the right questions about using social media for business: how to build trust and lasting relationships while building a community and how to make it profitable! If you read this book in its entirety and apply its advice, it will save you years of learning experiences and accelerate your success. Social networking is here to stay; it's no longer a choice when it comes to business and when you have an opportunity to learn systems that take you through the process step-by-step, you are blessed. Being in rooms for over three decades full of entrepreneurs there to be educated in advanced entrepreneurial skills, I can tell you from experience that even though many are already successful, they all want to find better tools, systems and ways to market their products or services. So do I... don't you?

Social networks have transformed the business world

It can look complicated, but no matter how much you may NOT want to get yourself and your business involved in this medium, I suggest that you truly explore it. Cydney O'Sullivan shares with you powerful distinctions, tools and systems that take the mystery out of what can look like a complex subject. You'll realize from this book that social media is just good business. You'll find that it can be easy, fun and profitable. I have known Cydney for several years and have found her boundless energy, humor, wisdom and ability to discover the right business solutions extraordinary. In addition to working with many major firms, she has successfully helped me with my business with wise advice and a clear desire to assure my success. She shares her contacts with ease and knows how to establish a relationship where all benefit. She is among the new leaders in Internet marketing and culture.

I congratulate you for reading this book. It will accelerate your business of the future, prepare you for greater success and assist you to create the level of wealth that you desire.

Dame DC Cordova
CEO of *Excellerated Business Schools®/Money & You®*
a global organization with over 80,000 graduates
from more than 65 countries. Because many of
today's wealth and business educators have
attended *Money & You®* her work continues
through them to millions world-wide.

INTRODUCTION

T he inspiration for this book came to me at a recent meeting with the CEO of a major media company. He confided that if they did not find a way to embrace the new technologies that have changed the playing field in his industry, his company would probably not survive another decade. The speed of decline of this company shocked me. In my lifetime, media outlets have been among the most influential – and wealthiest – businesses in modern society; just think Hearst, Turner, and Murdoch. But with the advent of the Internet, as well as the shift in advertising effectiveness and choices, the field has rapidly gone from mud to quicksand for many newspapers, business directories, technology providers and companies based on traditional media models.

Bad news for some, great news for others

Meanwhile, in the same economic climate, some of the people in my network have been making a fortune with the new social media while many of us are still tentatively dipping our toes in the waters. It appeared to me that if one could master the art of promotion on any one of Facebook, Youtube, LinkedIn, Google+ or Twitter, they could be staking a claim on a virtual goldmine.

I was retired, having made my fortune from the tech boom. But I lost much of my 'nest egg' in the fallout from the real estate bust. I was back in business helping clients create marketing campaigns for their books. I was finding that the world of publishing was changing dramatically and rapidly since my first book project with literary and publishing agents just a few years ago. Now the discussion was all about Amazon, Kindles and iPads.

Some of my associates were creating clever campaigns using emerging social business media, with staggering profits as a result. They were building targeted client bases in the tens of thousands in just days; and hardly any of it through the mainstream media that previously gave us our primary platform to the masses, our "five minutes of fame." The gatekeepers no longer control what gets public attention. The way news used to be released-'one to many'-is now a 'many to many' conversation.

At conferences I attended, however, it seemed that only a savvy few early adopters were getting these spectacular results and in fact most of us were still trying to decide if we could bother with, (or even should be on), these "time wasting social networks for the kids."

So I organized interviews with 30 extraordinary business leaders to find the underlying principles for successful social marketing. I was particularly interested in entrepreneurs from a variety of industries who were not only making a fortune, but also giving back as part of their business model and really leveraging the ripple effect power of the communities they'd built and nurtured. I asked them for their accelerated wealth strategies, and their best advice.

I was looking for the core, underlying values and beliefs that enabled these community leaders to flourish and prosper in difficult times, and the uncharted territory of the online age; the new frontier, where these very bright stars are creating *their own* media and social networks, some making millions at a time when many businesses are struggling.

I came to the opinion that Social Media Marketing is one of the greatest economic opportunities of all time.

There is a saying that your net worth is directly proportional to your network, and these days that is more measurable than ever. Now, with the emerging tools and strategies you'll learn more about in this book, you can expand your network faster than ever before.

I have structured the information so you can take immediate action from each one of the chapters that will make a positive impact on your existing business or help you create a great new one from scratch. Alternatively, you can power your way through the book, applying all the strategies and "go for gold," like I am! It comes down to how much you want your success and how long you want it to take.

If you want to access more of the interviews, or would like the audio and video tutorials, you can visit our website, www.MillionairesAcademy.com, where you will also find regular gifts, bonuses and updates to keep this information current.

I'd like to thank all the wonderful people at my publishers Morgan James who loved my project and encouraged me from concept to completion. My gratitude to David Hancock, mentor and visionary, Jim Howard and Rick Frishman who gave so generously their expertise and advice, Bethany Marshall and Morgan Toulouse for all the many day-to-day processes that make up a professional book of this caliber. Thanks also go to Bonnie Bushman for the fabulous formatting, and Rachel Lopez for the beautiful cover.

I owe a huge debt of gratitude to the legendary Jay Conrad Levinson, who now has taught me about Guerilla Marketing; along with Bill Gates, Steve Jobs and millions of others. I am also indebted to DC Cordova, the Grand Dame of Entrepreneurialism; the personification of mastery, resilience and commitment. So too, my editor Kathryn Calhoun who is not only brilliant, she has been there for me, through the ups and downs, and makes time in her schedule no matter how busy she is.

Huge thanks go to all the busiest people, who still found the time to review and advise on the book; Gail Oliphant, Peter Hoppenfeld, Brett McFall, Chris Gray, William L. Simon, Leon Jay, Sari Mustonen- Kirk, Michele Benson, Ardice Farrow, Judy Winestone, Clinton Swaine, Julie Mason, Dale Beaumont, Angelique Milojovic, Emily Graham, and Alicia Lyttle, I appreciate your input so much.

My inspiration and foundations I attribute to Jack and Suzy Welch, who have been kind and brilliant mentors and helped me streamline my focus and become organized, efficient and productive. Thank you also to Brett McFall who first introduced me to internet marketing and still guides me.

I also extend a resounding thank you to the brilliant marketers in this book, my mentors, who so generously shared from their experiences, donated their time to let me interview them for hours, and gave so much advice from the heart as well as their business success strategies. These experts were hand-picked for the incredible results they are achieving for their communities, and how they still manage to extend exceptional customer service while helping to add immense value to their networks and client bases. The incredible team at The Hunger Project inspire me to be a better person, and I hope you will be inspired too, please give generously as your success grows.

Lastly, thank YOU! I genuinely hope you get ideas, clarity, inspiration and bountiful wealth from your commitment to your success. Create your plan, see it through and take my advice and that of the great Jay Conrad Levinson; success is the result of laying the foundations and then seeing it through. Success takes patience and time, but I hope with this book, I can help light your path and clear the way. Writing the book and the accompanying training site was my champion challenge. Sticking with it will be yours.

With the impact of the Internet affecting most modern societies in a rapidly evolving business world, we have clearly moved from a transactional economy to a relational economy. Our experience of a business is a more important influencer than ever before. If we all competed on price alone, only a few could remain at the end of the battle. I think you'll understand when you read this book why I have dubbed this era the "Relation Generation."

How to use this book

I recommend that you read this book from beginning to end, implementing some of the suggested strategies in your business right away. I have created action steps at the end of each chapter that will help you achieve your goals and improve your branding, effectiveness and, ultimately, your profitability.

If you took on just one short chapter each day you could launch a new business or improve your existing one dramatically, in as little as 30 days. I encourage you to come back and then give each of the chapters much more time and attention.

As your business becomes more profitable, you should start to build your "dream team" – and that just might mean changes to your existing team. I recommend a system for regularly evaluating the fit and benchmark performance of each of your team members so that you can reward your champions while allowing the underachievers to move on.

This is especially important when you are employing contractors and outsource teams. Set realistic accountability targets and take the time to review those results. Be candid with your team; allow them time and opportunity to become high achievers, but replace them if they are not a fit. Provide an environment where your champions can also become millionaires and, in the process, turn you and your business into leaders in your industry. Have successors in line for each role, so you can adapt to changes swiftly.

Many of the contributors introduced advanced, accelerated wealth strategies based on their own experiences. The more in-depth tutorials from each of the contributors are at our site, MillionairesAcademy.com.

I would enjoy hearing how this information has worked for you! Please send your stories of challenge and success to inspire others to:

Cydney@MillionairesAcademy.com

Wishing you great prosperity and success!
Dream it! Live it! Love it!®
Cydney O'Sullivan

SECTION ONE

DARE

Don't worry; skills are cheap, passion is priceless. If you're passionate about your content and you know it and do it better than anyone else, even with few formal business skills you have the potential to create a million-dollar business.

– **Gary Vaynerchuck**, Author of *Crush It*
GaryVaynerchuk.com

CHAPTER 1

HOW TO BUILD A POWERFUL COMMUNITY

Sharon Pearson

Founder and CEO, The Coaching Institute, and Best-Selling Author

Sharon Pearson established The Coaching Institute in 2004, whose mandate is to facilitate the success of future coaches in a competitive marketplace. Her many business awards include the prestigious Australian Telstra Business Award, and the Victorian Business Woman of the Year. Sharon appears regularly on Australian national television and is the bestselling author of Simple Strategies for Business Success–How to Win the Game of Business and Live Life on Your Terms. Also, Your Success–10 Steps To An Extraordinary Life.

From misery to mastery

Where did I start? I started with nothing. I started in my bedroom with my dog and a box of stuff. I had no idea what to do next. I had no money, no clue, no clients, no community, I had no character. I was misery defined.

That seismic change in my life–going from nothing to multi-millionaire–happened because I applied the system I'm going to talk to you about.

We have clients who are doing million-dollar years using my formula. We just had a client tell us that he did $50,000 in the first two weeks of applying it, plus another has just had a $50,000 month.

So I get to have the dream. I get to spend the morning inventing stuff and coming up with ideas that are fun, and I've got $6 million in recurring personal income coming to me in the next 18 months. My businesses have generated over $35 million in revenues in the last five years.

The Coaching Institute is our biggest business. Combined, we do in excess of $10 million a year turnover and we make between $5 and $7 million a year profit. Last year alone, I personally donated a quarter of a million dollars to charities that are important to me. I became a successful author because of my businesses. Most importantly, I've got clients whom I really love.

I had no money, no clue, no clients, no community, I had no character... and I've got $6 million in recurring personal income coming to me in the next 18 months.

Find your niche

The first step to building a successful community is to go after a niche market where you can be perceived as one of the best in the world. That's not as hard as it seems. Some people may be reading this and thinking, "I'm not the best in the world at anything." Well, you're not... yet.

If you were to read ten books on the subject, help ten clients on that subject, find ten ways to improve your life or business based on the principles; you could be perceived as one of the best in the world. That's true for tomato growing, guitar playing, glass blowing and business coaching, for anything, if you just follow those three steps: read ten books, complete ten programs and implement what you learn until you get great results in your own life or business.

As a result of the principles that you're applying and believing in, all of a sudden your confidence goes through the roof and now you can position yourself as a world leader. To become the leader is not actually as hard as it seems. Most people buy books; they'll buy a self-help book to feel better about themselves, but most people don't read the book. They read the back cover and maybe a bit of the introduction, then they put it on the shelf. But they feel better because they've done something.

You've just got to finish the ten books and you're already way ahead of 80 to 90 percent of the marketplace today.

Define your niche

So you've gone after a niche market where you can be perceived as one of the best in the world, that's the first part. The second is how you define a niche. The more narrowly defined you can get that niche, the better you will do. You could be a coach for anyone–be a generalist–and you'll make $75 to $100 an hour and have some clients.

Or you could be a specialist coach in the field of business coaching and make $20,000 to $25,000 a month in income. Or you could be a specialist in marketing for small business owners with businesses up to $5 million; suddenly you've got a $3 million niche in its first year.

That's what I did. I went from zero in the niche of the Small Business Marketing Academy and the Small Business Mastermind Club to $3 million in just over one year because we applied this approach. We thought: we could be a business solutions provider for anyone and that we'd do okay. We could supply business solutions only on marketing and we'd do even better.

Or we could do marketing solutions only for small business owners who were business owner/operators in service communities. We did the latter and turned over $3 million in the first year. That's an example of the approach in action. When anyone says to me, "I'm thinking of going into this niche," these are the questions I get them to ask themselves:

1. Does it lend itself to a seminar where people would know why they're turning up and why it's appealing to them?
2. Does it lend itself to a bestselling book? If people bought the book, would they know what they were getting and why they've got to have it?
3. Does it lend itself to being able to make recurring sales over and over again?

There are my three requirements. If you've met those three, "Yep, I could easily fill the room because there are a bunch of business owners who are owner/operators who want to know how to maximize their Google spend," you're away. I know that's a niche. I know that will fill the room versus "I just want to help business owners with their mindset."

The next part is that the people in your niche have got to have a problem.

It can't be a bunch of people who are hanging out just for the sake of it. If they've got a problem for which they're desperate to get a solution, you're going to be much better off. It should be an inch wide and a mile deep, really narrowly focused to the solution.

The Small Business Mastermind Club is a small business marketing system for owner/operators who are experts; they're authors, coaches, consultants, trainers, seminar presenters or related service providers – a really narrow focus.

Most people do it the other way around; they offer something and hope enough people buy it. It's the whole "build it and they will come" mentality.

The people in your niche have also got to be willing to spend money on the solution. You've got to have people searching for the topic through Google. The number of Google ads really matters. If there are no Google ads in the niche, it's probably not a niche. Don't think, "Oh, but I'm probably the first to think of it." You're probably not.

Your target niche has also got to have a number of products to sell on the topic. If other people are monetizing it, you've got every chance of monetizing it. But you don't need to be the frontiersman about this to find out of it works. Don't be the guinea pig of a new market when you're starting out.

Know what your niche wants

You can't build a profitable business unless you know what your niche wants. This is where we're really getting to the heart of community. Most people do it the other way around; they offer something and hope enough people buy it. It's the whole "build it and they will come" mentality. It's: "I've got a cool thing. There should be lots of people who want my thing, because I really love my thing." And that doesn't work.

You've got to build your business on a hungry, starving crowd that already wants a solution. If you've got it that way around, it is effortless to do business every single day of the week.

The reason I know all this so well is because I've made every mistake possible. For two years I was trying to sell a product and it just wasn't selling. Just because

I believed in it and thought, this is what they should really want, doesn't mean that's what they actually wanted. They didn't.

It was only when I changed the offer completely by just shutting up and listening. I stood on the stage and said, "So what do you guys want?" And they told me. So I sold them that then and there and went and built the program afterwards. That's a true story. I did $100,000 that minute, whereas I had been struggling up until then to do $15,000 and $20,000. For two years, I had tried to sell the thing I thought they should have, but people don't buy what they should have – they buy what they want.

Once you've found and defined your niche, you need three Cs to build your business: Content, Characters and Community.

Content

Content is the least interesting part to your marketplace. Nobody is joining because of the content because nobody knows what the content is like until they've joined. You can't say, "I've got the best program in the world and that's why we do as well as we do," because nobody knows it's the best until they have it for themselves.

Your market doesn't want content; they want a solution. They want the results. So people will come for the content, but they will stay for the character.

The reason people join is because they come to know and love the characters in our company and the community we've built for them.

People come for the content; they *stay* for the character.

I've had a million dollar week because I cracked this code.

Characters

What are characters? It comes out of defining your clients or customers. You need to define who they are and then go on to build a "character" or the "characters" that will drive your business.

First of all, who is your ideal average client who loves you, loves what you offer, keeps coming back, raving fan and who you're always on message with because who you are and what you offer is exactly what they're wanting?

There are three types of clients you have: the client you're working with, the client you think you're working with and the client you wish you were working with.

For a long time I *thought* I was working with clients who were into building a successful coaching business. Who I actually was working with were clients who just wanted a community.

Once I got clear on my ideal average client whom I could best serve, I started having million dollar–literally, I've had a million dollar week–because I cracked this code. So the three questions you should ask yourself are:

1. Who do you think you work with?
2. Who do you really work with?
3. Who do you want to work with?

Talk to your clients. Ask them questions. Here's a sample conversation:

Me: "What are you enjoying about the program?"
Them: "I really love hanging out with people and all the chats. I really like everyone."
Me: "How are you doing building your business?"
Them: "I didn't do it for that."

I'll just do it for person after person. I shut up and listen to their answers. I thought I was working with a client who was a go-getter. I was actually working with someone who was not. I thought I was working with someone who was into building a business and making money from this, but I wasn't.

So I started marketing to the person I actually had. Suddenly sales went through the roof.

Creating a character or avatar for your business

If you could manifest a person who would be the embodiment of your classic client, who would that be?

Get clear on that one person and–this is really important–stop trying to market to a bunch of people and from now on only market to that one person.

So when you send an email, do a blog post, you're writing only for her. If you try to appeal to everyone, you'll end up appealing to no one. You'll be so watered down and so beige, and beige is death in business. Now, because we only attract people who are like this character, we only have people who are raving fans. Our complaint rate is less than one percent.

The power of characters and your community

Using characters is powerful because it reaches to the core of people. It's not about products.

People want to belong. They want to be plugged in to an elite community. We all believe we're special and unique and people crave the opportunity to have that "Significant Special Thing" noticed by someone else. If it's noticed consistently, if you keep lighting it up, they should stay in your community.

That's where it begins. It's the recognition that people want to be seen as specific, that they matter, that their life has meaning and that you will be the vehicle for fulfilling that dream, that potential within them. And that's at the core of creating a successful community.

The moment you try and compete on price or on discounting, everything I'm teaching goes out the window. Now you have to move volumes to monetize, which means you'll take anyone, which means you'll appeal a little to a lot and you won't appeal a lot to anyone.

Social marketing and the community

I'll write a blog and then I'll have people in our community comment on the blog. My blog posts typically receive 50 to 100 comments. It's me saying, "I've got this great blog. I'd love to know your thoughts. I'd love to get your feedback. Let's get a conversation going." And I start a conversation going around the blog. That builds community.

With emails, I'll send an email not just teaching something—which is content—I'll reveal some of my character in it. The emails are written fairly irreverently, but bluntly. I'll share great value but I'll also ask for feedback, which is another way of building community.

On Facebook you can friend me or The Coaching Institute, it's the same thing. Actively we're posting photos, ideas, quotes, sharing what's happening in the latest training. It's building a community that way.

We send newsletters every single week to our clients, personalizing moments that are special to our community. We run webinars and teleseminars all the time. For our students, they run almost every day. For our prospects, it's once or twice a month. We make sure we touch our members or reach out to our members every single week with classes, emails, Facebook, a phone call, a note in the mail.

So knowing your community, your character and constant contact are the keys. So, bottom line, "Everybody else tried to sell me content, you guys just let me hang out with you and get to know you."

That's it. That is how we monetize it.

Cydney's Social Wealth Action Steps:

1. Define your niche. Where can you be perceived as one of the best in the world? What niche is narrowly defined and has an eager market with purchasing power?
2. Do the research: what is the problem your niche wants solved?
3. What other products are for sale in this niche? How do they compare to yours?
4. What does your community actually want?
5. Who is your avatar? Define your ideal client.

CHAPTER 2

DEVELOP 360°
RELATIONSHIPS

Dr. Lois Frankel

Founder and CEO, Corporate Coaching
International, and Best-Selling Author

Dr. Lois Frankel, President of Corporate Coaching International, works with multinational corporations including BP, GE, KPMG, National Australia Bank, Nestle, Proctor & Gamble, Microsoft, Warner Brothers and Goldman Sachs. Her books, Nice Girls Don't Get the Corner Office and Nice Girls Don't Get Rich, are international bestsellers translated into over 25 languages worldwide. She is one of the top names in international public speaking and has also authored Stop Sabotaging Your Career, See Jane Lead and, most recently, Nice Girls Just Don't Get It (with Carol Frohlinger, JD).

Dr. Frankel's television appearances include The Today Show, CNN, Fox News and Larry King Live. She has also been featured in USA Today, People Magazine and The Wall Street Journal. Lifetime Television, in conjunction with Drop Dead Diva producer Josh Berman, has purchased the rights to Corner Office for a comedy series. In addition to her work as a consultant, keynote speaker and author, she is the founder of two nonprofit organizations, MOSTE and The Bloom Again Foundation. She has been honored with numerous awards for her work empowering women and girls.

From corporate to coach

From the time I was a teenager, all I could envision myself doing was being a psychologist. In preparation for my dream career, I earned a B.A. in psychology, an M.A. in counseling and a Ph.D. in counseling psychology from the University of Southern California (the latter by going to school at night while working full-time in human resources at the oil company ARCO). Soon after receiving my doctorate and becoming licensed as a psychotherapist, I left ARCO to start my own private practice of psychotherapy.

But life has a way of throwing us curves. About a year and a half into it, I realized I wasn't cut out to be a therapist. It was the moment I wanted to jump across the couch, put my hands around my client's neck and scream, "How many times are we going to talk about the same thing?" that I thought I should be considering an alternative career.

It was the moment I wanted to jump across the couch, put my hands around my client's neck and scream, "How many times are we going to talk about the same thing?" that I thought I should be considering an alternative career.

About the same time I had a client, who I had done some consulting for, call and ask, "Lois, would you be willing to coach someone?" This was over two decades ago and you have to remember that at that time there were no business coaches. I had no clue what I was supposed to do. When I asked my client, she said, "You've worked in human resources, you've done training, you're a psychotherapist–put them together and you have a coach." Figuring it had to be better than being a therapist, I gave it a try and soon learned coaching was really the perfect place for me. It allowed me to use my education, experience, skills, interests and relatively high energy level. But it never would have happened had I not built a strong relationship with this client who was often ahead of the curve in so many ways. She trusted me to "get it" and when I did she rewarded me with many coaching clients at a time when I really needed the work.

Soon I was coaching full-time, but realized I was never going to get rich this way. When you're a solo practitioner, you can only do as much work as you have time during the day. So I came up with this concept for team-based coaching.

Clients were often referred to me who had multiple development areas and I didn't always have the expertise needed to address every issue. My vision was to provide each client who needed it with a team of coaches, each with unique skills from which the client could benefit. I called on people in my network to explore how we might work collaboratively, and here is where we really start talking about the critical importance of having a broad network and strong relationships. As I often tell people, when you need a relationship, it's already too late to build it.

When you need a relationship, it's already too late to build it.

The result of that initial meeting with colleagues who had backgrounds in psychotherapy or other helping services, advanced degrees and experience working in-house at corporations led to the formation of Corporate Coaching International. As far as I know, it continues to be the only team-based coaching company in the world. But without my already built network, I wouldn't have people upon whom I could trust to serve my clients well.

Relationships have always been important in business, but especially now, here in the United States, where we have seen volatility in our economy. What I have noticed is that when people are laid off or have to close their businesses, those who are most successful in quickly getting back on their feet are the ones that have the relationships already in place. They can call on someone and say, "Hey, I have to be honest with you. My business isn't doing well and I am wondering if you know of anyone who is hiring or people who could use my services." If those relationships weren't in place *before* the economy turned, it would be much harder and take a lot longer to climb out of the hole.

We all need to build strong 360-degree relationships all the time. By that I mean with people who may be senior to you, peers, people who report to you and even outside vendors. You continually build relationships–even with people you think you would never need anything from–because you don't know which one you'll need in the future. Let me give you an example:

When I worked at ARCO, there was a woman in another department who was junior to me. I think she had graduated from high school, but she had no college education. Each year, in our departments, we had to do a report for the government that was quite complex and, frankly, not a lot of fun to do. It was very hard for her and every year she came to me and asked, "Lois, would you help me with my report?" I helped her, not because I ever expected to get anything from her, just because it was the right thing to do. Well, I left ARCO to start my therapy practice and on the side I was doing corporate training. One day the phone rings and it's this woman. She said, "Lois, I just wanted to let you know that there's a woman from Indonesia who is coming to town and she's looking for trainers to bring to Indonesia to facilitate management and leadership development classes. If you're interested, I'll introduce you."

Even though I had no clue where on the map Indonesia even was, I said, "Sure, I would be interested!"

That was about 23 years ago and, to this day, I go to Indonesia several times a year to coach and train Indonesian nationals. That relationship with someone, whom I'd never thought I would hear from again, has brought me hundreds of thousands of dollars over the years. So that's another example of how critically important relationships are.

> I tell entrepreneurs all the time that building
> relationships is equally if not more important
> than offering high quality services or products.

360 Degree Relationships

To get the full picture of what I mean by 360-degree relationships, picture a bicycle wheel with all of the spokes coming out from the hub in the middle. You are at the hub of that wheel. The spokes represent the various relationships that you have. It could be with peers, bosses, direct reports, clients, and colleagues from professional associations or with vendors. All of those spokes that come out represent a different group of constituents and you need to build and manage *all* of those relationships. If you don't think you have to build relationships with vendors; then listen to me, because I'm a vendor to a lot of clients. When they don't treat me respectfully, they don't get the best service that they could. If you think of me and treat me as a "vendor" then I'll treat you like a "client" and not a trusted partner for whom I want to do my very best.

I tell entrepreneurs all the time that building relationships is equally if not more important than offering high quality services or products. I offer to help people at no charge just because it's the right thing to do, not because of anything I anticipate receiving in return. Yet I've learned that the more you give, the more you get back. It's not always from the same person you gave to, but what goes around comes around. Certainly I don't think I've ever done something thinking, "Let me do this because this person is going to help me someday."

I've learned that the more you give, the more you get back. It's not always from the same person you gave to, but what goes around comes around.

It's really about a generosity of spirit. When you are going to build your brand, whether it's your personal brand or your business brand, you have to include a generosity of spirit. This lets people know that you're not just in it for the money. When I wrote my books I wasn't in it for the money–most authors will tell you you're never going to get rich writing a book. It certainly has added to my financial portfolio, but that was never the intention. The real intention was to help people who may never get coaching or advice otherwise.

Remember, you're in the middle of a very complex network or a web of relationships upon which you depend to be successful. You depend on all of them. To survive you also need to stay networked into what's happening in your industry, or what's happening in your field. Once you think that you have it, once you think, "I've got this down, I don't have to go to networking meetings, I don't have to join professional associations, I don't have to read books," you are going to make yourself a dinosaur.

Similarly, you have to stay in the loop with what is happening with technology. Some companies that went belly up are not in existence anymore because they didn't change with the times. They thought, people are always going to need us. A good example is Kodak. Even when it was clear that digital photography was taking over the field, they continued to focus on making film. Their business has suffered tremendously as a result. So you need to stay connected in all ways with people and events and technology in your field.

The power of branding

Branding is critically important and many people overlook the importance of it. Do you know why we buy a brand over the generic? Whether it's Coca-Cola or Kleenex; we buy a brand because we know it, we trust it, it's consistently reliable, it's marketed well, it has a cachet to it and it has a kind of quality associated with it. So those are all things you need to think about in building *your* brand.

I was on a radio show the other day and a woman called in and said, "I have a child care business and really want to know how to get more parents to bring their children to me."

I asked, "What makes your child care services unique among all of the others that are available in your community?" There was silence on the other end of the line. Finally, she admitted that she couldn't tell me what differentiated her services from those of others. Until you can do that, you can't build your business because your brand has to have something that is unique and that customers or clients want to buy. What makes my coaching firm unique is that we are the only coaching company that provides team-based coaching. We work on all of a client's development areas because we don't want them to have a hole in their skill set.

Relationships are not only important to you personally, but also to your brand. People do not buy your product, they buy *you*. Yes, your product has to be good, but that's a baseline. Why should somebody buy Corporate Coaching International's consulting services over some other firm's services? Well, if my services are great, as I am sure many other companies are, then it is going to be because of a relationship built on mutual trust and respect. That's part of the brand.

Something else that goes along with branding is that your brand has to be, look, feel and sound high quality. For example, when I first started my business, I created high quality marketing materials. Back then you had to have hardcopies of everything. So, at a time when I could least afford it, I put a lot of money into an identity kit, brochures, letterhead and so forth that looked like they were coming from a Fortune 500 company. I had worked for a Fortune 10 company, so I knew what quality looked like. If I was going to be marketing to large enterprises then my materials had to look just as good as theirs. That's going to be their first impression of you.

Nowadays, I tell people that their websites have to be outstanding. When I go to a website and it is average, I kind of assume that I'm going to get average service or an average product from the person who has that website. So when you start building your business, you need to think about how you are going to invest in branding, whether it's on the website or in other forms of advertising. When I see people's business cards they have printed off on their own printer, it rings a bell for me that this person either isn't investing in their company or don't think they're going to be around that long; they don't think it's important. I'm looking for quality; we're *all* looking for quality when it comes to how we're going to spend our hard-earned dollars.

> When I see people's business cards they have printed off on their own printer, it rings a bell for me that this person isn't investing in their company; they don't think it's important. I'm looking for quality; we're all looking for quality when it comes to how we're going to spend our hard-earned dollars.

When they pick up my materials I've heard people say, "Wow, this is a really slick brochure!" That's exactly what I want them to say. Think about what you want people to be saying about your brand as you start building it. I want them to say, "You know her brand is high-quality all the way! She doesn't skimp." Because then they know you're not going to skimp when it comes to providing them with your product or service.

Relational influence

I founded my first nonprofit organization, MOSTE (Motivating Our Students Through Experience), when I was working for ARCO. Its mission is to provide mentors to inner city schoolgirls who are at risk. Most of these girls come from families that are living at or near the poverty level. I started it because I believed if we wanted a diverse workforce of the future, then we needed to ensure that these girls stayed in school, didn't join gangs, didn't get pregnant and went on to college. They didn't have role models at home for how to be a high achiever. If you can't see it, you can't be it.

It was about pairing a young girl with a woman in business who could just show her the ropes. Sometimes it's as simple as showing her how to go out and eat in a restaurant or, if you go to a museum, what should you be doing? What should you be looking at? Through this kind of exposure, young women gain self-confidence. But where was I going to find the mentors? I started calling my counterparts in other large companies in Los Angeles and found nearly 20 women who were willing to join me in this effort. They each enlisted a few of their colleagues and pretty soon we had over 50 mentors. Now, MOSTE has been around for 27 years and has in excess of 100 mentors. I'm very proud of having been a part of its inception.

About six years ago, I was diagnosed with breast cancer and was treated with surgery, chemotherapy and radiation. For about a year I could only work at my own pace because it was a pretty grueling regime. One day when I was sitting home, I thought, 'How lucky I am that I have my own business? I have financial independence. Not every woman is in the same situation and when I'm finished with all of this I'm going to help women who are not as fortunate.'

When a friend came to visit and my hair was starting to grow back in, she remarked, "It looks like you're blooming again!" Bloom Again became the name of the foundation I started as a way of providing financial assistance to working women who live at the poverty level when they experience medical emergencies. For these women, one missed day of work is the difference between paying the rent and being put into a shelter.

I couldn't have founded Bloom Again alone. Here again networks and relationships come into play. I called on eight women, some friends and some colleagues, with diverse skill sets and interests and asked if they would be on the board of directors. To my surprise, every one of them agreed and together we forged a path, a vision, and a process for helping women in need.

Just today I received an email saying, "Could you help this woman? She has seven children; her husband is in jail for domestic violence. Because of the domestic violence she gets these headaches and keeps missing work. She's behind on her rent and utilities." They were only asking for $700 to pay back rent, utilities and some other things. I sent it to the board for a vote and in less than four hours the Board of Directors voted in favor of helping her.

Bloom Again helps women to get back on their feet and become financially independent by taking one more worry off their plates so that they can heal well. I'd love you to visit our website, www.BloomAgain.org, and to friend us on Facebook http://www.facebook.com/bloomagain.

Cydney's Social Wealth Action Steps:

1. What is unique about your business that you could leverage?
2. Review your branding. Does it send the right message?
3. How effective is the relationship management program in your business? List ways you could improve it and take steps to implement those.
4. What communication channels do you have in place for your team to improve your business?
5. List 10 connection techniques you will add to your operations to develop your 360-degree relationships.

CHAPTER 3

YOUR SOS PLAN FOR SUCCESS

Sir Kenneth Miller

Founder and CEO, Global Marketing Group Ltd and SanteVu LLC

Ken Miller is a marketing innovator with a specialty in residential and resort development. His company helps plan and create the project concept and then manages the marketing and sales. Based in New York, his clients include developers, governments, financial institutions, Fortune 500 corporations, ITT, U.S. Steel, Chase Manhattan Bank, Hovnanian, Maxxam, American General Insurance, Morgan Guaranty Bank, the Sheraton Group, Interval International, J.C. Carras, Daito Kogyo, AGA and the United Nations, among others.

He has been responsible for several billion dollars in sales. Miller maintains his international contacts and is currently working with projects in the U.S., Caribbean and Asia. Working with the United Nations, he founded the National Committee for Habitat to help families worldwide obtain affordable and sustainable housing.

Relational marketing—the foundation of social business

Our firm has a database we developed over the years through our network of professionals involved in the full cycle of real estate: the banker, the developer, the broker, accountants, architects, planners and lawyers. If you're in that cycle, we want you to know that Global Marketing Group exists, wants to help you and wants your business.

Over the years we used all the standard media to promote our clients' products. We were among the first to use television as a technique to promote retirement housing in the New York area via innovative, humorous TV commercials. We created our own media via sponsoring property expos in London and cities worldwide. For years we published an e-newsletter, "SOLUTIONS for DEVELOPERS," which reached our database of 40,000 real estate professionals.

Now prior to recommending any media to a client, we explore everything regarding social networking and LinkedIn. We insist, or we literally walk out the door, that our clients first have a realistic marketing plan before they consider bringing their project to the marketplace. We recommend our firm prepare a simple but awesome marketing plan we call our SOS Plan: "Situation, Objectives, Strategy" (not to be confused with "Save Our Ship" or others).

We advise that before your firm ventures into the marketplace, you prepare a simple, realistic and doable marketing plan. Our formula can be used for any business. What is your situation, what are your objectives and what is your strategy to achieve those objectives? This can be 15 to 50 pages depending on the complications of the product or service, but until you prepare this plan you should *not* invest another dollar. It has been said, "Invest your time before you invest your money." Only that approach assures the best potential for success.

Invest your time before you invest your money. Only that approach ensures the best potential for success.

Let's use real estate as an example:

- Situation: What is your competition building that is similar? What are the pros and cons versus your competition? What are local salespeople saying about that particular project? Who is buying and at what price point? Is financing available and on what terms? Only after extensive discussions and research, prepare this aspect.

- Objectives: Given the information above and realities of the times, what are achievable, realistic and defendable objectives, short and long term?
- Strategy–the fun part of the SOS Plan: determining the strategy to achieve those objectives based on the situation. Once the team is on board, a realistic marketing budget is stated and part of the strategy. Given that we know our buyer profile and objectives, we now can get a peek into the media to consider, but even before that part of the marketing strategy is finalized, many other aspects need to be determined. One, for example, is how important is adding a brand? If you're a developer without a known brand name and you're seeking the highest possible return, you might want to add a brand name to flag your property.

For example, a five-star hotel flag may make an arrangement with you if your property fits their criteria. They most likely have a fee to use their name and a charge per unit sold. Evidence illustrates the possibility of getting higher prices and selling at a quicker pace offsets the extra costs involved. I believe in most cases it is worth the extra dollars (insurance) because it will reduce your marketing cost. More people will be favorably impressed to visit your property, be less inclined to cancel and have a higher comfort level. Also, buyers will most likely have an easier time at resell.

When we prepare the strategy aspect we seek to discover the unique selling proposition (USP). For example, what is unique about "Sydney Acres?" Is it the location, amenities, eco-development, health amenities, golf course, spectacular views, great spa, etc.?

The media mix

After all that and more is accomplished we determine the media mix, which would likely include online and offline media to reach the prospects cost-effectively. If you invest $1,000, how many phone calls, visits or clicks are you going to get for that? It's an important point.

Lastly, what's needed is a great website. Right now, in real estate, 85 to 90 percent of every sale starts with a click. You go to their website, review all pertinent data and if you are interested you will proceed with an additional click, a call or a visit.

The two main differences now are the social networking media and the requirement of having a great website. Those are things we didn't have in the past, but we're very in tune with now.

When we develop a specific SOS Marketing Plan, we make it as simple as possible so all involved can easily follow to assure the best chance for a successful venture.

An example of an SOS plan in action

One client, Chase Manhattan Mortgage and Realty Trust (CMART), presented us with an interesting challenge regarding a resort they owned on the island of Puerto Rico, a four-hour flight from New York City and two-hour flight from Miami.

CMART, together with other banks, lent in excess $100 million. The money was lent to a developer who created a destination resort on a 2,700-acre site with two and a half miles of beach. The developer built 21 tennis courts, a golf course, marina, 750 condominiums, 3 restaurants and a boutique hotel. The project was ambitious to begin with and when the market softened, a property recession occurred and the resort could not deliver the cash flow necessary to be liquid. CMART took the property over from the other banks and retained my company to explore 3 scenarios: sell the project to an investor, bring in additional developers to build more products and determine if timesharing of the unsold 125 of the 750 condos was feasible. We prepared three separate SOS Plans:

SOS Plan #1: Sell to one developer. This was almost successful; we discovered via our plan a major U.K. airline ready to purchase and build out the resort. In addition to owning a great resort, another motivating factor was they wanted to establish Puerto Rico as their gateway to South America, but technical issues caused the buyer not to proceed.

SOS Plan #2: Attract developers to build more condominiums, hotels or home site projects. This was successful and eventually four European developers purchased parcels and built new products. What sold the international developers was creating compelling reasons why Palmas del Mar was the ideal place to build a new and profitable resort property.

Working with Palmas architects, we planned 22 developer parcels on the 2700 acres, each with a specific use. We did the research to determine which developers worldwide would most benefit by owning a parcel. Given Puerto

Rico was going through political tension at the time that was much publicized in the United States, U.S. developers were ruled out as prime investors and European developers were determined to be our best opportunity. We discovered comparable parcels on the Rivera were more expensive and took more time to obtain approvals. Thus we were confident we would attract developers from Europe. We then created the tagline "Palmas del Mar, The American Riviera."

That tag, the comparison of the Caribbean side of Puerto Rico with the Riviera, created some controversy. To prove our claims to international developers, we prepared the answers and a compelling presentation to prove it. The strategy program was extensive and successful.

SOS Plan #3: Timeshare the unsold condominium units. We determined the local market was ideal for the summer weeks and off-islanders for the balance. The timeshare program was a success and created a good cash flow. We sold out the initial units and built another 25 units to timeshare.

After a few years, Palmas del Mar, Puerto Rico became one of the most successful resort developments in the Caribbean. It was a spectacular turn around and prime example of how a success can happen with a realistic marketing plan and brilliant execution.

Ken's success tips

Some tidbits I learned to attain success are:

- Do the best you can each and every time.
- Stay in direct contact with your clients, ask them what you can do, maintain the relationship. This relationship building will lead to good will and only good will happen.
- Love what you do, learn about it, become an expert in what you do so you can share with the leaders in your business. Explore writing articles, speaking at seminars and perhaps writing a book.

We take our own advice and we are launching a new wellness/health business and I am writing a humorous health book on that subject. I know it will be the key to our success.

Social responsibility

Social marketing is how a company gives back. There are many spins on the technique but in the end I discovered that must always be a part of your marketing plan.

Social marketing is how a company gives back.
There are many spins on this technique but it must
always be a part of your marketing plan.

Every company on Earth should create a fund that part of their profit goes back to doing good just for the reason of doing good and for sure, doing good for others will always do good for you. It is the proverbial "win-win situation" that really works.

Cydney's Social Wealth Action Steps:

1. Prepare your own SOS Plan.
2. Schedule a meeting with your management or mastermind team to map out your SOS Plan and identify opportunities for promotion.
3. Allocate a team member to undertake research to help you understand what your competitors and other companies in your niche are doing to improve their client attraction and retention.
4. Run surveys to get feedback from your existing and past clients to know where you are strong and where you need to improve in your client experience.
5. As a team and individually, identify some key growth opportunities for your business that you have not been pursuing with the vigor they merit. Set up some action steps to activate those opportunities; delegate and set milestones and target dates.

Note: By now, you should be looking at how you can leverage your social marketing efforts in a socially responsible manner, with the end goal of creating a positive impact and fostering goodwill in your community.

CHAPTER 4

HOW TO MAKE MILLIONS ONLINE

Armand Morin

Founder and CEO, Armand Morin
Network, Inc.

Armand Morin is the founder and CEO of Armand Morin Network. A self-made multimillionaire, Internet strategist, author, marketing authority and recording artist, Armand is one of the foremost Internet marketers in the world today. Having started online in 1996, his personal online businesses alone have generated over $85 million in revenue. Type "Armand Morin" into search engines and you'll find his name is on over two million websites. He has helped thousands of people in all walks of life to increase and enhance their online businesses through automation and his highly acclaimed "Generator" brand of software, which has been used by tens of thousands of people in 101 different countries. He's taught thousands his unique and proprietary Internet business-building principles and strategies, as well as his unconventional, no-nonsense life design and management skills.

Internet marketing: the early days

In 1996 everyone said, "If you're going to do any kind of business, you have to be on the Internet." I took that pretty seriously, so I started looking around. I didn't know anything about computers; I didn't know anything about the Internet. I didn't have a technology background.

That's where I started from. I saw things that people were doing online. One of those things was selling a link on their website. They said, "If you give me $20, I will put a link on my website, I'll get a bunch of traffic to my website and therefore you'll get traffic to your website."

I thought that was a brilliant idea. This was literally the day I got on the Internet, so I was going to do the exact same thing because it looked like it was working. I found this little course, AOL Press, which promised if I followed their directions I would have a website online in just a few hours.

I followed their directions and sure enough, I had a website online in just a couple of hours. On my website I said, "If you give me $20 I will put a link on my website." I just started advertising it. From day one, I put up a website on the Internet, started advertising it through classified ads that I found on AOL and in that first seven days I made $8,000 all in $20 bills! That showed me the Internet could work.

The first week I had over 1,000 orders and at 12 weeks, I had over 36,000 people giving me $110 each; we had brought in $4.2 million.

From that time we started developing products. If I had problems, I would come up with a solution, create it and market it to other people. A lot of my earlier ideas were software, for example "eBook Generator." In the beginning of my Internet career, I was very fortunate because I had this simple idea. I collected all kinds of bookmarks for my website, meaning anything I found that I had an interest in I would bookmark it on my browser and I organized them all. My idea was that other people would find those bookmarks interesting as well.

So I started selling my bookmarks in a simple membership site. Then I would charge people $110 to access my bookmarks for a year. The first couple of days I started advertising it, we had 100 orders–about $11,000 of income in the first 2 days! The first week I had over 1,000 orders and at 12 weeks, I had over 36,000 people giving me $110 each; we had brought in $4.2 million.

At that time we were using a lot of classified ads on the Internet and I was smart enough to put together an affiliate program. That's how we were advertising. It really wasn't anything major. Google wasn't around, Yahoo! was barely there and didn't even have an advertising program. We were shut down after 12 weeks because we processed too much money in too short a period of time. I knew that company I had was going to do about $155 million in sales that year and because they had taken away my merchant account—my ability to take credit cards—I had to find another way to accept credit cards on the Internet without having a merchant account. I did some research and found out there are these "third party processors," which meant that I could use their merchant account to process my orders.

I found about 80 of them and wanted to list them in an e-book. Back then, e-books weren't as prevalent or in the format they are today. We put the information together and I needed e-book software. I bought software and none of them did what I wanted my book to do. I decided, "If someone could create software that did all of these things I want it to do, I bet they'd make a fortune. Why can't I do that, aside from the fact that I don't know how to program anything?"

I hired someone, they put together the software and we still market it to this day. We started creating simple software to allow people to do some of the things that I was doing on my websites and we still do that today, even with some of the newer products that we develop, for example, "How to Write a Sales Letter" and "How to Create a Website."

The problems that people are having on the Internet, the questions they ask each and every day; if someone creates a simple solution to help them, people are willing to pay for that.

That's really the secret to Internet marketing success. It is solving the problem that someone has. If you have a solution, then people are willing to pay for it. The more difficult the situation they're in, the more money people are willing to pay for what you have.

Your online business

Start off with your own website first, that's the very basis, the core of being on the Internet. That's where your focal point should be. Once you have that, the type of business you are will be determined by what you do on that website. If you're a consultant, then your online strategy is to get more people to hire you as a consultant. If you sell products or services, your objective is to get people back to your website to buy. If you sell information, whether it is physical books or digital books, then your objective is to get them to your website to buy your book.

You have to have a core idea of what you're trying to do. Create the website and get that running. Then define what your objective is, and focus on that.

How to make a million dollars

If your objective is to make $1 million, figure out how you are going to get there.

- What's your product?
- Define exactly how many of those products you need to sell.
- Create a marketing strategy in order to sell those products.

If we use some average numbers we can figure out where we need to be. Let's assume we have a product that costs $50. Out of every 100 visitors that come to your website (use some really low numbers and say that 2 percent of the people would buy), 2 out of every hundred, would mean 2 percent equals $100. Now we find out how much traffic we need in order to make $1 million dollars. A million visitors times 2 percent gives us 20,000, times $50, and that gives us $1 million. So, if you show your offer to one million people, at a conversion rate of 2 percent, and a sale price of $50, your total sales equals $1 million.

Find your flagship product

A lot of people have a line of products. You have to have what I call your flagship product, meaning the thing you are known for. That should be the one promoted most heavily on your website.

One way to figure that out is what do you do most in your company? What do you sell the most? What do people actually buy the most from you? Also, what do you make the most money on?

A lot of companies want to sell product A, but in reality, the majority of their money is made when people purchase product B. They're promoting A, but they should be promoting B because that's where they have the most profitability.

Social media and your website

You have to have a clear understanding of what you're trying to do with social media, a lot of people think that it's separate from your website.

The whole objective behind social media should be to direct users to your website. If I'm on Facebook I want a reason for people to give me their name and email address so I can communicate with them outside of Facebook. If I'm on Twitter, I want people to give me their name and email address so I can market to them outside of Twitter.

The whole objective behind social media
should be to direct users to your website.

What's been happening lately to a lot of the commercial marketers is they've been getting cut off from YouTube. They've been getting their accounts shut down. YouTube is not a commercial platform and they have programs and strategies for commercial applications. With your basic YouTube account, you're not supposed to promote products and/or services on it.

Give people great information, whether it be posting to your Facebook page, Twitter, Google+ or whatever it may be. Then drive them back to your website where you can market to them.

You don't want to sell through Facebook. You want to give them a reason to want to click through. The more great information you give them, the more they're going to follow you, and the more they're going to tell other people about your posts.

Think about everything you post as being its own little, mini viral campaign that people will want to automatically share with other people, getting more people to follow you and building your bigger social media campaign.

Social media strategy example

Live on stage, I created a fan page on Facebook for Justin Bieber. The goal was to prove how quickly you can do it, and in less than 48 hours we put over 114,000 people on it. Now it's up to 176,000 without me touching it.

What do you do with it? I can market to them, I can say, "I found this great thing, take a look." They click on it, go to a website, if they like it they can buy.

We do CPA offers; someone might put up an offer that says: "Win a Free iPhone." I send out this offer, saying, "You can win a free iPhone. Here's a link."

If someone enters their name and email address, I might make $1.75 to $2.00 for each one of those.

Each time we send an offer like that to a list of, say, 50,000, we'll get from 200 to 300 per day people actually take up the offer. We typically make from $400 to $600 per day in that type of scenario.

These are fan pages, so we're not trying to impersonate a celebrity. We're just saying that this is a fan club about this individual and then promoting products that are related. Also, I promote my main fan page for my business and siphon some of those people over to my business, which is really where I want them.

Lists: the secret to social marketing

The key is your list. When I say "list" I use it in the broad sense, meaning your email list, customers, people that follow you on any social network. The bigger your list, the bigger your business is going to be.

When you're building a social media campaign to build a list, in some cases, you actually have to advertise. One of the attractions in social media is that you can build a list for free. Technically that's true, but it's unrealistic to some degree.

One of the attractions of social media is that you can build a list for free. Technically that's true, but it's unrealistic to some degree.

A better way is if you advertise. If I advertise my Facebook page and get people to like my page, I'm actively building a list and that's more people I can market to. It's about getting more people to see what you have, whether you're doing that by email or by social media. Every person you add is adding to the list of people you can market to, that you can instantly communicate with.

Affiliate marketing is the greatest form of marketing. If people are willing to market your products and services for you, they're going to spend their money on ads. They're going to send it to their lists, and you're going to reach people that you never thought possible through your affiliate network. By building your own affiliate system into your product or service, you can really expand and leverage all of their connections and all of their resources unlike anything else.

Affiliate marketing is not only very popular nowadays, but by giving people the right tools you can make it easy for them, especially if you have great products that people actually want to buy. If people don't want to buy your product, then you can have all the affiliates in the world and nobody's going to make any money because no one's going to buy anything.

You need to have a great product, always, from the start. Also, give the affiliates the tools they need. In our affiliate program when a person signs up to market our products and services, we break if down for every single product that we have. We have a regular link, give them two or three different emails that they can send out, about ten different banners for each product, pre-designed Twitter and Facebook messages and pre-designed Google ads they can run.

We don't leave anything to chance. It's already pre-filled out forms, so they literally just have to copy and paste what we have. That makes it easier for us to market the products.

Measure. Measure. Measure.

We use a lot of analytic software on our websites. We measure everything you could possibly imagine. We use Google Analytics, which is a $6,000 software that Google gives away for free. The capabilities are vast. Most people only use it to gauge how many visitors came to their website and maybe where from, but it does so much more.

How can you improve what you don't measure? If you want to improve what you're doing on the Internet, gauge exactly what you're doing, whether it be running ads or changing your website in some way and you can see if it's profitable.

Tip: a simple way to track is to sign yourself up as your own affiliate. Then you advertise. Every time you create an advertising campaign you advertise under that affiliate link. If that affiliate link gets sales, you know that advertising worked. You know how much you spent. You know how many sales you got. Now you can tell if it was profitable for you or not.

Success tips

If I had to do everything all over again, what would I do differently? I would do things that have more continuity built in. What I mean by that is I would create more products and services that people pay for not just once, but they pay me every single month for.

If you had a product that you sold for $30 and 100 people buy that product, that's $3,000 worth of income. If you had that exact same product set up as continuity where people are not only paying you $30 once, but they're paying you $30 a month, now we just turned that into a $36,000 a year income. The question is, what can you market to people that would be worth $30 *and* would be worth $30 every single month to them? That means you have to provide some worth every month, and that's good.

You get paid, not just from one person, but from other people too. Each month that is compounding, meaning you're getting paid on your existing 100 people, but also any new people you bring in. Now you're building a residual income. In any country anywhere in the world, look at the biggest companies, and you'll find that those large corporations have some sort of residual income attached. They have customers paying them month after month for a product that typically they deliver one time.

What can you deliver? For the average small business, the easiest thing you can deliver is information. What changes that people would want to know about every month, where people would be willing to spend $30 to learn more about it? How much information should you provide to get that $30? It really depends upon your industry and your market.

Success online

Three key ingredients to my success online would be: I'm not afraid to make a mistake – I know I'm going to make mistakes and not get everything right the first time; number two, I'm very persistent and don't give up easily; the third thing is you have to be optimistic. If you're a negative person, if you're a pessimist by nature, you probably should just get a job. Being an entrepreneur is probably not for you. No matter what the situation is, how dim it may be – and you will have some dim times and grim times being an entrepreneur – you have to be optimistic through that, knowing that you're going to be able to get through and there's light at the end of the tunnel.

You're not going to have all the answers all the time. I don't. That's okay. Does everything go exactly the way I plan? Absolutely not. But do I keep on pushing through? Yes. Do I keep on trying to learn new things? Absolutely.

Cydney's Social Wealth Action Steps:

1. Who are your ideal high-spend, long-term clients?
2. What magazines and websites are they checking out regularly?
3. Where could you promote your offer, (once you have tested it and have it creating sales), that already has an audience of your ideal clients? For our recommendations on advertising media, visit www.MillionairesAcademy.com/Resources/Advertising.
4. Delegate one of your team to contact these media and prepare a report listing their advertising rates. Remember to ask about any special promotions coming up that might be highly targeted for your offer and attract your ideal clients.
5. Conduct a survey with your list to identify problems that you could solve. For examples and survey sites we recommend, please visit www.MillionairesAcademy.com/Resources/Surveys.

A Wealth Acceleration Note From Cydney:

After Armand's interview I came up with this formula to help with my advertising goals:

I'm assuming the goal is to make one million dollars with a $50 product, as in the example. If you advertise the offer to one million people, and two out of every hundred buy (2%); that equates to 20,000 sales at $50 each, which totals $1,000,000.

(As a frame of reference 20,000 sales in a year equates to about 365 sales per week)

So the formula to help calculate your required target market exposure is:

Target Market Exposure *(TME)* = Revenue Goal *(RG)* / Product Price *(PP)* / Conversion Rate *(CR)*

TME = RG / PP / CR

So, as an example, to make one million dollars in sales with $100 product:

Where RG = $1M, PP = $100, CR = 2%
The TME = $1M/$100/2% (0.02) = 500,000 you should aim to reach

Average weekly sales at 2% conversion = around 192 sales of $100 per week

So, if the cost of advertising online was $2,000 per 100,000 of your identified target market, then would you now potentially choose to spend $10,000 to make sales of around $1,000,000?

Of course, as in any business, conversion and 'stick' rates are dependent on and affected by many factors; the market demand, relevance, quality and desirability of your product, effectiveness of your offer, deliverability and service.

CHAPTER 5

HOW TO BUILD A JUGGERNAUT OF A PROFITABLE BUSINESS

John S. Rhodes

Creator, Juggernaut Product Series

John S. Rhodes has published over 100 books. He left his job as a Software Engineering Executive for a Fortune 500 company, managing multimillion dollar projects for some of the world's largest businesses, when his online side-business was absolutely exploding. John created, built and then sold his first marketing business around 1998, in his early 20s. It was profitable within two months, with no debt, and eventually became so successful it simply made no sense financially to stay in his day job. With one of the first 1,000 blogs on the Internet, he has consulted with several of the world's most respected and profitable Internet marketers. John is the creator of the Juggernaut series of information products, helping others create their own "bone-crushing" profit solutions using SEO, article marketing, list building, niche marketing and much more. He has an Associate's Degree, a Bachelor's Degree in Management Science, and two Master's Degrees: one in philosophy, computers and cognitive science; and one in cognitive and behavioral psychology.

Your business is you

I had a six-figure job and my pay was rapidly increasing, but I had a six-figure business on the side as well and, eventually, every hour I was at my corporate job I was losing money. I've got a wife, a couple of kids. I'm conservative with my money, for the most part. I do some things that are risky, but I plot, I plan and I look years ahead. I'm a long-term strategic thinker, so the building of my community is in line with my personal values.

I talk to people about their businesses, where they have been, where they are and where they are going. The thing I like to stress is that your business, for most people, is *you*. If you're not true to yourself then you're done, you're sunk. If you don't know who you are, then you can't be true to yourself. You want to be the best you that you can possibly be. The world is getting more biased in favor of entrepreneurs. Look at the ability to outsource (and be a freelancer on the other side of it). Look at the enabling power of technology. If you don't know yourself, then you don't know what to outsource. You don't know what you are strong at or what your weaknesses are. You're trying to do everything. If you try to do everything, you will fail! You need to know who you are, what your value is, and that you're going to repel, literally repel people! They will hear you and they won't like what you say; they won't like your voice, your positioning... But you're also going to bring in the people that are aligned to who *you* really are in your core.

The thing I like to stress is that your business is you.
If you're not true to yourself then you're done, you're sunk.

Set short-term goals that align with your long-term strategy

Here is what I do: I go to a lot of events and speak at a lot of them. Before I go to the conference, seminar or gathering, I find out who is going to be there. I find out what the purpose of the event is, I learn what this event is all about. There are actually two pieces to this, that's sort of the background phase. Then the very, very first thing I do after I collect that background information is I decide what my number one goal is for going. Even though I'm being paid to speak, or going to be the keynote or I'm going to run a workshop, I still go there with a purpose. I'll turn down speaking engagements that pay–and even pay a lot of money–if they don't fit with my overall long-term business strategy and what I really want to get out of life.

I will pick one specific thing; it could be striking up a conversation with someone else and getting their contact information or setting up a joint venture with them. In other cases, it's to get across a certain point to everyone and get everyone in alignment. I might be collecting email addresses or doing a case study and want feedback from everyone. So imagine the satisfaction; I go, I do my speech and I accomplish my one single goal, and then everything else is just wonderful. I can relax.

So, I know who is going to be there, but what are they going to be talking about? What's their purpose, in general? Then I specifically focus on and define one goal. One very specific tactic I use that has been extremely effective is for every single conference, every seminar I go to, I get a brand new business card created. These cards are specifically focused on my goal and they are in the context of the seminar or event that I'm going to.

Here is a specific example: I went to a small invitation-only event with between 80 and 100 people there. Every person in that room had a business generating over $1 million in revenue, and some of them many times that amount. So, I created a business card that was oriented towards those million-dollar businesses and a brand-new simple website ahead of time. That website was all about supporting and providing services to million-dollar businesses. My business card was all about providing white label and private label products, services and support for million-dollar businesses. So people got my business card and went, "Wow, you couldn't be in a better place!" or "This is so specifically targeted!"

In many cases when I go to an event, I will create a new website and new cards, and that's the business card I hand out. People are always blown away at how direct, relevant and targeted my business is to their needs. I have many systems, tactics and processes that I use to build businesses from scratch with certainty that they're going to succeed. Remember to build businesses around people, your marketing, your business cards and your websites around people. If you do that you cannot go wrong. You will always provide massive value and you will always make money. If you're creating value for the sake of other people, you cannot go wrong. So I just reverse engineer the situation and say, "Okay, what are they there for? What's their number one need? Number two need? Number three need?" I go after one of those and literally build businesses from scratch.

I know what my strengths are, so I capitalize on those strengths and then repeat what I do, again and again, and evolve as I go and continue to use what works and get rid of what does not work in my marketing.

The Warrior Forum

I'm one of the top sellers on the Warrior Forum because I'm ridiculously prolific. I've put out 20 to 30 products this year. The Warrior Forum actually is a forum; like when you think of bulletin boards and forums. It's the biggest Internet marketing forum that I know of. There are over 330,000 registered members, even though many never show up. But you're talking about tens of thousands of people that are coming on and off the Warrior Forum in a day, tens of thousands! It's insane how much traction the Warrior Forum has.

There are a number of different subsections. For example, you can go to a classified ad section, a joint venture section, hire people to do work for you, there's a copyrighting forum, a pay-per-click section, search engine optimization area, AdSense and more on top of that. Releasing that number of products that are super high quality obviously gets me a lot of fans and loyalists.

People are always blown away at how direct,
relevant and targeted my business is to their needs.

Finding great resource providers on the Warrior Forum

That's one of the ways I get so much done. If you're looking for people who are especially technical and marketing oriented at the same time, you can find very good resources that I actually recommend to people. It can take some time, but it's worth it. There's one gentleman and all he does is guarantee that you'll get to the first page of Google for one of five or more keywords that you give him. Any keyword! It can be *any* keyword. If he doesn't do it, he just keeps trying. He's an example.

Build your business around your unique strengths

My unique ability is that I'm a "maximizer." If you give me something, I can maximize it. It doesn't matter if you're a speaker, have a great product, great business, joint ventures, copywriting or you're great at interviews, I can help you do better. Very often when I talk to people they will say, "John, you just changed everything for me. You literally changed my life." That's my unique ability.

My unique ability is that I'm a "maximizer."
If you give me something, I can maximize it.

When it comes to my specific "technical" skills (I use that loosely!), I do the copywriting for email, sales pages, I always copywrite. Even within my products I always build in a certain level of passion and enthusiasm because that's part of my specialty. I drive that into my products. I teach other people how to do that as well. If you can do that, if you can drive yourself into your product and your passion and energy, then you're going to do really well.

Social marketing and selling

For me, social marketing is not about selling. There is some marketing in there. I try to position myself a particular way, to make sure that the information I'm giving people is personable. I try to let people know that I'm a real person and that brings me closer to a lot of people. By being human you also resonate with people; you're not really selling. You're able to get word-of-mouth advertising, build joint ventures, connect with people and that means referrals a lot of the time. You actually have a built-in social network of reputation managers at different levels helping you out and they connect you to other people they know. I don't even try to make money or sell anything through Facebook; the idea of selling socially doesn't work very well.

Understanding people and mailing lists

People say, "John, how can you be so prolific?" One of my tactics is to understand who I'm going to talk to, remember psychology, remember usability, remember to build things around people, build businesses, your marketing, your business cards around people, your websites around people. If you do that, you cannot go wrong.

With mailing lists, you're going to have three types of people: the first group is the prospects. They have never bought anything from you. The second group are your customers, the first-time or one-time customers; they buy and now you know they have a pulse, they're interested in what you say and they've proven it by spending some money. Then, you have your repeat customers and loyalists.

You have these three different groups of people and how you market to them really depends upon what you're trying to do with your business. When it comes to research, think about what that means. If you blankly ask your whole list a question, put a survey out, you're not going to get results that really make a whole lot of sense. Do your research in a relatively focused way. At least break up the non-buyers from the buyers if you're trying to figure out what people want, what they will buy again, what price points make sense and so on. That information alone will save you a lot of time, money and aggravation.

Tips on expanding your team

Look at the people in your own sphere, people you know, people who are already on staff, connections that you have, partners, joint-venture partners, maybe even affiliates, people on your list and see if you can find people that can do the work that you need to have done. Then you can offload that work from yourself, they take that work on because they are already doing it, they already enjoy it, and you're getting their passion and their talent. You're in a chiropractic office and you find out that this person who is already on your staff is great when it comes to online stuff and they love this Facebook and Twitter thing and LinkedIn, and they get it.

Then, you look at what they've been doing; find their lowest-value activity and outsource that. So you take someone who has talent, passion and skill in some area; you allocate them, offload their work and then you're getting rid of the lowest value work, that's what you outsource. So you move down that chain and everyone benefits, you benefit, your existing staff benefits. This is how you can justify giving people raises because they are providing more value to your business. This is truly revolutionary for a lot of businesses.

Accelerated wealth secret:
Create and release a brilliant training program

The first thing I would do is understand what value I can provide in a market that has a lot of money, is very active and is very interested in buying something

I know about, something I have some skill in. If I had money to invest, I'd get more creative and add in software and plugins. Then, I'd put together a training course that is of ridiculous value, I mean just flat out ridiculous value.

Then, work with the key players in your industry; you can do the webinar circuit, meaning you can go from one person to the next who is in that niche and get them to promote you. They make money; you're doing affiliate marketing, joint venture marketing.

Take that training program and maybe some software that you have and bring that to the market through joint venture partners who are already well connected, already have lists, already have a Facebook presence; and piggyback on their traffic, their reputation and their presence. The tradeoff is you are helping to make them rich as well, helping them grow their wealth.

You contact these people and bend over backwards to help the best of the best, even by giving away most of your profit. Once you've done that you have put yourself in their league. Then you can reach out to more of their peers, reach out to people with smaller lists and continue to do that. That positions you as a "guru," gives you a lot of fast free cash. It allows you to build your list, build relationships with the strongest people in your industry. You rapidly become a mover and shaker.

Release a monster training program in a niche that is very hungry, that has a lot of money and work with key partners. That's what I would do.

Cydney's Social Wealth Action Steps:

1. How efficient are your client and prospect communications systems?
2. If you don't have one already, choose an emailing and customer relationship program and set up an account. For systems we recommend, visit www.MillionairesAcademy.com/Resources.
3. What high-quality, high-value offer could you make to engage with your mailing list?
4. Should you write the offer? Is there someone more qualified in your team who would be more reliable in creating your ongoing communications? Set out a simple plan and include regular follow-up.
5. Brainstorm and then delegate the creation of the offer; set a timeline, due date and launch date. If you do not have in-house service providers to assist with your marketing collateral and content creation,

visit our recommended resources at www.MissIndependence.com/ Services, the Warrior Forum or one of the many outsourcing agencies we discuss throughout the book.

CHAPTER 6

SYNDICATE FOR SUCCESS

Jennie Armato

Founder and CEO, Web Business
Academy

Jennie Armato is a best-selling author, public speaker and mentor. Her books include Web Entrepreneur Millionaire, Return from Adversity: Inspired Entrepreneurs and The Law of Alignment. She is a creator of programs that educate and empower entrepreneurs who want to lead. Her signature programs include The Entrepreneur Super Star Success Master Plan, 120 Days to $120,000 and the Shine Online System.

My journey to conscious marketing

I've been in my own business since 1992. I grew up in a family-based business so I guess it was always in my blood. I got on the Internet in 1996, started selling online in 1997 and have been on social media since 1999. I've been using the personal brand of "Australia's First Lady of Social Business" and have two education-based organizations: The Web Business Academy, founded in 2004, which helps people get online or get their businesses to new levels online; and The Conscious Entrepreneur Academy, which looks at social business and conscious entrepreneurship.

People get lost in the online world in business when they go to a particular tactic without understanding the wider implications and broader picture. I don't see myself as a consultant but more as a practitioner; I teach what I've learned. People master the theory of something, but it's quite different how that translates to the business bottom line. A lot of people don't know what the endgame is in business and I think why we have such high failure rates. I'm looking for multiple bottom lines in my business.

Whether you're in business or working for a cause, charity, non-government organization or non-profit, you are selling something–communicating an offer to help people move forward to a next step with you and, in business, intentionally becoming your customer, then from there potentially becoming your lifetime client.

The future of selling is what we call the "online marketing channel." You can't afford for people to ever say, "I couldn't find you on the Internet." If you ever get that feedback, get some help and get optimized, because somebody's being found for whatever it is you're selling and someone's going to get the sale.

> You can't afford for people to ever say, "I couldn't find you on the Internet," because somebody's being found and someone's going to get the sale.

The online channel

I've broken down the online channel into three groups. This is in one of my blueprints, called "The Future of Generating Website Traffic Easily." All are essential to building a sustainable business, in keeping your marketplace happy and in keeping your pockets happy.

Group one is the search engines. A search engine produces a set of results that take you to pages based on the keywords that you've searched for. Group two is the spender engines: websites like Amazon, iTunes and eBay where people go with credit card in hand, ready to spend, looking for products specifically. Group three is the social engines. This is where people go in search of other people that have what they want. The social engines include Facebook, Twitter and YouTube; those are the most popular, but there are hundreds of them (and there's a top ten that I'm going to introduce you to in a bit).

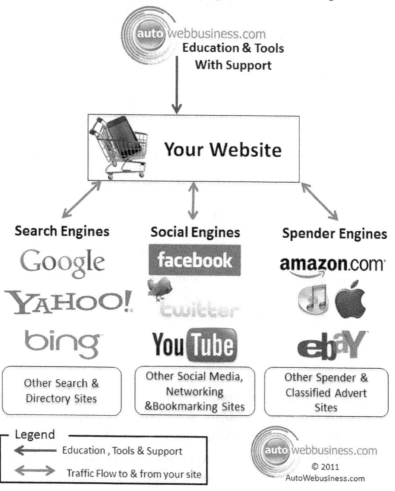

THE FUTURE OF GENERATING WEBSITE TRAFFIC EASILY

How your Website, Experts and Traffic Sources Work Together

To have adequate online channel coverage going forward, have your business functioning in all three groups. These channels bring us leads on keywords we want people to find us under, because they're highly qualified, or warm, leads.

There is still value in offline marketing. We do telephone marketing. It's a very effective way to reach people; we use it for sales and servicing. We use Skype so that we can operate our business internationally and we still use old-fashioned snail mail, not to negate the value of email or mobile marketing because they're still valid.

However, the future of selling in the most efficient and powerful way is online. It's not just getting a website and putting something on Google; it's having adequate channel coverage across all three groups.

The most powerful place to build your profile and presence is on the social engines. There's this concept that we're shifting from a targeted market to having a broader conversation with a wider audience; the "word of mouth" is now the "world of mouth." Third-party referral is what I call the "engine room" of social engines. People will share your content, even if it's not for them, they'll follow you, they're interested in who you are and what you do. They'll share what you've got to offer with people they know. The people who frequent these websites are social by nature and they're like a free army of people who will carry your message and deliver it to your market.

We're shifting from a targeted market to a broader conversation with a wide audience; the "word of mouth" has become the "world of mouth."

Imagine if I could cast my marketing net wider than my current reach and directly to my intended market. Imagine if other people would willingly circulate my information for me; they're not making it up, they're simply passing it on. Imagine if I could go from a local business to a global business for virtually free. There are just over 800 million people on social engines every day and it's growing. With Internet coverage globally of over 75 percent, there's a lot of growing still to do. I'm happy with 1 percent, even 0.1 percent of people picking up my stuff and sharing it until it hits the people that are genuinely interested and qualified for what it is I do.

"Auto-Magic" content syndication

There are ten services that are going to give you the most leveraged power using the social engines; they'll allow you to build your profile and presence and predominantly build it automatically. I like to call it "auto-magically" because you can write a simple blog post and through automated technology syndicate it across 10, 20, 30 sites all in the blink of an eye.

Your content can be delivered across a massive network literally using automation. The ten services are:

1. An RSS feed–"RSS" stands for "really simple syndication." This tool acts as a syndicator. If you don't have a blog structure on your website, now would be a good time to organize that.
2. The Google Profile is a key element to linking Google to the social engines. It allows you to put links on Google to all your social media or social engine presences.
3. YouTube is a video platform. Generally you can make a three- to five-minute video; it could be explaining how to use your product, talking about something exciting you've got coming up or anything you want. They'll host and promote for free for you.
4. iTunes has the same technology as the RSS feed. You're able to hook your website straight into iTunes. If you were to produce any audio or video content that is not loaded on YouTube, you can run your own radio show through iTunes and open up that distribution channel as well. It's free to do; it's called podcasting.
5. Twitter is an information network where people tweet short messages with links.
6. Facebook is a social network. Facebook allows both individuals and businesses' professional profiles to showcase themselves and connect with people.
7. LinkedIn is the professional network. If you're targeting a B2B audience you're more likely to find your people on LinkedIn.
8. Flickr is a network for hosting images so it's an excellent place to upload anything visual. It could be photos about your products and services if you do events.
9. & 10. The last two, Digg and Delicious, are "bookmark" sites, news summary sites. When you do something like a blog post on your website, you can add a bookmark to it on Digg and Delicious. If people search for the keywords that your article or blog post is about, it can come up through the network. Journalists search for stories in the Digg network because it links to articles and they are

sorted by topic according to the keywords that you use when you make your articles.

I want to mention another site: Ezine Articles. It's not a social site, but set up an account with them as well. You can take something that you have put on your own blog, tweak it so it's a new version, put it on Ezine Articles and have a massive syndication as well. It's another great way to get your content out automatically and further than you could ever sit and do manually promoting. If you're going to produce content that's information-based, you may as well have an Ezine Articles account and let the power of the network and syndication work for you at the same time as you're doing stuff on the other sites. The interesting thing about all the sites is that they interconnect with each other.

That is probably the most complete beginner's package for social websites. One of the best ways to get started is to find other leaders or peers in your target market, or your industry, that are already active. Learn from them and what they're doing because chances are they get the game.

Syndication setup

Step one is to set up and activate with these different profiles. Behind the scenes, they all talk to each other, they update each other and do the most incredible things.

The devil's in the details, getting these accounts set up, getting them completed; you do need to micro-manage it because this is your whole marketing view. Remember, there's a potential audience of 800 million people. You can pay someone, a virtual assistant-type person, to set it up for you initially, but go back over everything yourself.

Set up your website, set up your Google Profile, then depending on your target audience, start then with Facebook or LinkedIn. Integrate the others as you go. Get one set up well and move on.

You can customize your YouTube channel to match your branding. It gives you branding recognition so that people have a consistent experience across your different websites.

Open a YouTube channel and shoot a quick video. Open your Flickr account and upload a couple of pictures of your products. Fill in your Google profile with some basics. Always think like this: What would I want the decision-maker of my ideal client to see if they come looking for me? Then start connecting with

THE NEW BUSINESS ECONOMY STRUCTURE

How your Weblog Feed + Search and Social Engines Work Together

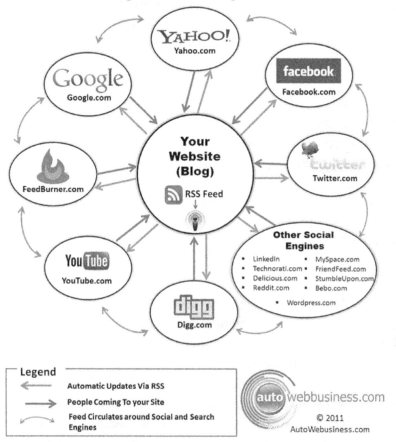

people. Because you've got these profiles complete, people can find out about you and even refer other people to you without you doing anything. You put the networks to work for you.

Always think like this: What would I want the decision-maker of my ideal client to see if they come looking for me?

Keyword research

Step two is keyword research, which is an imperative part of getting a good social engine strategy set up, just like on the search engines.

Search for the keywords that you think people would search for (for you), then on the results of those searches look at what other keywords people use. Google has a fantastic free keyword tool; just search for "Google keyword tool." You can get great related searches, too. You might have two or three keywords and the keyword tool gives you another dozen.

Google Analytics tell you what people use to search for your website. Most webmasters will be able to tell you what your searches are through the stats collected on every website. You can access them through the control panel and see historically what people have used. If you're sophisticated and monitoring your landing pages, you'll know what keywords actually converted into sales. They're your gold keywords. They're the "keys to the kingdom."

Once you've got your profile activated and you're connecting with people, you're keyword-rich, the third step is to create content and actually get that ready for distributing.

Content

Writing and producing for the social audience is different from writing for a sales brochure. It's definitely more conversational and more informal. It still needs to be purposeful; you've got to know what your objective is for writing it. But people want to feel like they're reading something that's personal.

Another difference with writing for the web is people don't read a lot any more, they scan. So it's a different writing style and keywords are key.

The content you write must include a call to action. This is the bit that people miss. Have a landing page on your website that relates to the content you're putting out to be syndicated. The call to action can be to buy a product or a service from you or to opt in to a mailing list. Also, on your landing pages have the ability for people to share or "like" your page.

People are putting content out and it's not purpose-based. They're not going to improve their bottom line. It's not leading people to somewhere that is specifically designed to bring them into your sales funnel. So be very clear about your objectives. Make sure that the content that you syndicate takes people back to a page that is all about taking them to the next step with you.

Multi-sensory engagement

How do you want to produce your content? You can do it as print format, blog posts, as audio or as video. The best format by far is video because it's the most versatile. You can extract the audio track from it, turn a video into a podcast on iTunes. It's much easier sometimes to show and tell; it's the most popular form of education and entertainment online today. We make video and then turn it into audio and we turn it into print or text content as well, so we're getting three levels of sensory engagement.

Your site

Don't send people to a general homepage. Send them to something that's specific and related to the content you've put out, so you can take them to the next step and that page is set up properly. "Properly" means that if it's got a product offer; it's got a "buy now" button and it takes them through an ordering process. If it's an opt-in, then it has an opt-in box and a reason that I'd want to give you my email details to get on your mailing list. It also has the ability for me to say, "I like this page," on my Facebook and on my Twitter.

Social selling

I've gone from what I call a "one-dimensional bottom line" of only thinking about profit, although we still love that, to a "four-quadrant bottom line." The purpose of my business is my contribution to the planet, it addition to profit. Business plays a big part in our day-to-day lives, so it had better be fulfilling.

Social selling comes down to developing a powerful profile and presence. The good news is that most of the profiling can be done automatically and therefore it can be quite efficient. Social selling has three key elements:

1. The Marketing Mindset Shift. Your business is now broadcast, producer and presenter, not just a product with a brochure. Your business has more meaning today to other people. They're interested in who you are and what you do, not just what you sell.
2. The Strategy Shift. You are now addressing an audience, not just your target market. So it means using to your best advantage that these people listening to you, who may not buy from you but who are now going to act in your favor if they like you, help promote you 24/7 around the world.

3. The Activity Shift. We still want strategies and selling systems on our websites, but the top of the sales funnel has expanded. There's more to your business than your products in today's world. People buy not just products; they also buy from whom they remember. Often business is picked up in the referrals arena not necessarily because you may be the best, but because you're the one everyone remembers who does that thing.

So what starts out as a blog post can now travel across all of these social sites and reach people in all corners of the world. We're now these mini broadcasters —like a mini TV station or radio station. That's what's available to us when we understand and embrace the idea of social media.

Accelerated wealth secret:
Cause marketing

"Cause marketing" is a strategy I'm using to differentiate myself in my very crowded marketplace. It allows for people to get on board with businesses like mine who want to promote a cause. People who support the cause will easily and happily share the fact that you're a part of it and that makes people want to support you even more. That support is priceless.

One of the things I was able to introduce into my social marketing or selling was sponsoring or funding entrepreneurs through an organization called Kiva, a micro-finance organization. People like you and me can fund or loan as little as $25 to people in underdeveloped countries and actually help them grow a business. It's a collective of you and me and 20 other people each loaning that person $25 to give them the total sum they need. Through the Kiva system it gets paid back through the lending company and then back into our individual Kiva accounts, so we can re-loan the money.

It's a beautiful cause and Kiva is tuned into the social scene as well. I was loaning, people were seeing that I was loaning and starting to ask questions. So I set up a team on Kiva where people could loan with me. Now I'm finding loans on Kiva where they might have $200 or $300 left; I'm loaning my $25 and then I'm putting on my Facebook and Twitter, "If you'd like to also loan to this person, here's a link. They only need a couple of hundred more dollars." We're now completing these loans for people. It is wonderful and the message of what you do is your magnet. I'm able to make a difference in the world and, through the social scene, help other people make that same difference in other people's worlds. It makes people want to do business with me more.

I'm not doing it just for that reason, however. I was talking about multiple bottom lines, the sense of fulfillment and purpose that I didn't have in that one-dimensional model of just thinking about the profit. It's really changed my life and it's made me want to be a better person, a better business person and it's really made me want to make sure that the eulogy of my business is one that people stand up and sing praises to. It's been a really wonderful way to be a more complete person as a business entrepreneur, what I'm calling a conscious entrepreneur.

It's important that we feel good about what we do, good about our lives, our bank accounts and what you can do to make your world a better place. By being profitable you're actually able to make other people's worlds a better place. The biggest disservice you can do for people in poverty is to be poor yourself.

Cydney's Social Wealth Action steps:

1. Prepare a professional profile package with a short, business-like biography, a longer version of your biography, a headshot and a list of your accomplishments. This can include career milestones, awards and certifications, etc. Create a descriptor for yourself and/or your business that helps people understand at a glance why you are unique. Examples are "The Career Coaches," "We Move Dead Inventory," "Reduce Your Overheads Specialists" and so on. Tags like these can be very effective on social media profiles.

2. Set up one per day: your professional Google account, Google+, your YouTube channel, eBay profile, Facebook page, Twitter and LinkedIn account profile.

3. Create professional content for Ezine Articles (EzineArticles.com), Digg, Amazon, Kiva, StumbleUpon and Google Alert accounts.

4. Link each of your accounts to each other. For instructions, visit www.MillionairesAcademy.com/Syndication.

5. Delegate a member of your team to create a bank of short and long articles that you can start posting to your various profiles as weekly updates.

CHAPTER 7

MAXIMIZE FACEBOOK TO INCREASE YOUR COMMUNITY AND SALES

Jim & Emily Graham

FB Cash Creator

Jim and Emily Graham are the founders of FB Cash Creator. They are leading Internet marketers, focusing on automated Facebook solutions including lead generation, offline-to-online transitions for small businesses and individuals, product launches and affiliate marketing. They provide customized Facebook fan pages optimized to grow email lists, sell products and drive traffic. They also provide a multitude of trainings to empower people to take better control of their Facebook communities.

Mega-industry, mega-growth

We started our Internet business in 1999 on eBay, earning hundreds of thousands of dollars and have been recognized as eBay Power Sellers. We studied under the top Internet marketers and since 2008 have been international speakers on Internet marketing topics. Recent successes include the launch of FB Site Creator, a product co-produced with Steven Essa, which allows you to quickly make unlimited fan pages in Facebook, and FBResponse.com, which auto fills email opt-in forms using Facebook connect programming to build powerful lists of email addresses easily.

As of March of this year, there are almost 2.1 billion users of the Internet worldwide, and almost half that number on Facebook. It's growing at a rate of 20,000 new users a day and last year, there was just over $165 billion in revenue from the Internet. That was up 14 percent from 2009, even though there was a global slump. It's projected to grow at another 14 percent this year.

Where can you have a 14 percent increase in revenue in any type of business where you are relying upon others? The answer is not many places at all. The other part of this is that when there are 20,000 new users of the Internet coming on every day and they're into Google, Bing, Yahoo, Facebook or they're putting up their first blog with WordPress, these are opportunities because these people want information.

Here's another statistic: 44 percent of Internet use comes from Asia; almost 23 percent from Europe; 13 percent from North America; 10 percent from Latin America; almost 6 percent from Africa; 3.3 percent from the Middle East; Australia and Oceania, 1 percent. Your customer is probably not in your country, not on your continent. Your customer is everywhere else but home. So please open your mind and think about it. Think globally, not locally.

Your customer is probably not in your country, not on your continent...
open your mind and think about it. Think globally, not locally.

For 10 years we had a carwash and our goal every day was how do we get more traffic? How do we get one more car a day or one more car an hour, to have more revenue? Online, it's the same thing, except our buildings are websites. When we got into the Internet business, we were intrigued by global revenue, something that's becoming more important as the world's economies change. Having a global revenue stream, we have so many potential buyers. If we can find more buyers with the same amount of effort, we have more revenue.

A complete marketing platform includes authority websites, sales funnels, membership sites, list-building, affiliate systems and then also putting it all together to get traffic. Most people we meet hire a web designer; the challenge is that most web designers have limited experience with making a website that can make money. They may make a beautiful website, but they don't have any idea how to make that website get an email address from a potential buyer or actually sell something on that web page.

We have one client that spent over $40,000 in 2 years with a website and had only $29 in total sales. Her site was beautiful, but it's like a beautiful car: if that car won't start and we can't drive it, it doesn't do us any good.

Niche

Pick a niche. Choose something that's related to your passion, that you're interested in and this will make it more exciting and enjoyable. Go to magazines, book stores, find out what people are talking about, if there's niche market potential.

Identify salability: will enough people want it that I can sell the product? Google has a tool that allows us to do this for free, the Google keyword tool. With the same tool we can find the strength of competition rating and that'll tell us how many competitors are in that niche.

If you can find a need and fill it, or find a problem and solve it, or find a want and complete it, we now have a value proposition. The next part is to find out income potential. We can have a wonderful niche, but if there's no money in it, it doesn't do us any good. We have to ask ourselves, "Is this something people are willing to pay for?" If we can answer "yes," we have potential income.

People are people. When we go into a store locally, we're going to buy from someone we trust. Online we have to convey the same type of trust with our web page.

When we go into a store locally, we're going to buy from someone we trust. Online we have to convey the same type of trust with our web page.

Dominate multiple keywords in your niche

You have to have Facebook if you're going to be an authority in a niche these days. Here's a tip: Facebook fan or business pages are quick to create using a multiple of different keywords to dominate your niche. If you have no money you can easily create pages and link them to other social media tools and create a machine driving traffic to wherever you want to point it.

The great thing about social media today is that you can now integrate many different engines to all automatically post to each other providing control to each other.

Handy Facebook tools

Facebook tools are important to keep people engaged on your Facebook pages. Some of the ways to do this are:

- Status updates: One post, whether to share information, or to sell something, can reach all of your fans.
- Facebook albums. Facebook is largely about the pictures. You can create graphics that sell your product or service with a call to action and then link the product to a sales page in the comments section.
- Facebook events: events are great for driving traffic to your website, fan page or product sales page. You can invite friends, other Facebook pages, and groups.

The Facebook page features you should have are:

- You can have a website inside of your page by creating a custom page and adding to it. Anything you can have in a website you can have in a Facebook page. This is an opportunity to build your list, sell your products, embed videos and much more.
- Import an RSS feed to your Facebook page "Notes" feature and whenever there is a new article on that website, Facebook will automatically create a post and a note from your RSS feed.
- "Tell your fans" is a really cool feature in Facebook that allows you to upload a .CSV file of up to 5,000 email addresses and suggests people to like your fan page. Set up your fan page's default landing page tab to your custom page; this way you can control what non-fans see first.

We personally do all the above on every one of our fan pages.

Posts

This is the one thing that we think a lot of people have trouble with, but you have to write posts. You want to keep your content fresh, original and engaging.

You want to portray on your fan page that you are an expert on your subject matter.

The problem with writing is twofold: many have trouble writing fresh content all the time, so we can supplement our own by buying prewritten private label rights (PLR) content. There are PLR articles we can buy to start with and then modify so it's more personal. You can take sentences from these prewritten articles and create posts from them.

The other challenge people have is writing posts that encourage interaction from the fan page community. If you ask a question, make sure it's open-ended and not too deep a question. You could ask people to fill in the blank, for example: "Fill in the blank: I never thought I would _____..."

By creating posts that get interaction, Facebook will rank your fan page and your posts higher so more people will see your future posts and your page when they search on your niche. This is what Facebook calls "edge rank."

Product

These are things we can sell from a Facebook page:

- E-books: Sometimes known as "the miracle product" because it's information, easily downloadable, easy to buy and it works really well.
- Audio: The next step up from an e-book. You can record anything. If you make a webinar presentation you could record the audio. You can do podcasts on iTunes, they sell for more than an e-book. Audio is wonderful if you have some expertise, passion and knowledge to put out there.
- Video: The most effective way to tell a story. High impact, higher perceived value, more detailed information. Video and audio together equals more information in front of the customer.
- Software: One of the highest potentials for profit, create it one time and sell it over and over again. It's easily downloadable and has high perceived value. There are potentials for upsells, add-ons or new versions.
- Physical products: Something that you can touch and feel. You can find things to sell at Disk.com, CreateSpace.com and Alibaba.com. Alibaba.com is a resource to find almost anything in bulk for less cost. These are items that also can be drop-shipped. You don't even have to worry about the inventory in a lot of cases. You take the order, send the order off to

your supplier and they'll ship it for you. If you don't want to create your own product, Clickbank.com is a great resource to find products to sell in almost any niche.

- Services: Coaching, copywriting, webinars, design, consulting, etc. If you can run a webinar or can do coaching from home and put it out electronically, you don't have to have an office. You can outsource a lot of the work.

Make sure you test your sales process. Split testing allows us to know what's working and what isn't.

Accelerated wealth secret:
Add upsells and downsells into the sales process

You have your main Facebook page, maybe there's a one-time offer, maybe there's an upsell, maybe a downsell. It doesn't really matter, but there's a process and there's technology out there that can help with that to make it simple.

When we determine an upsell, we want to have an offer for the buyer after they've agreed to purchase. This increases revenue and profit. The downsell is offering a cheaper alternative when somebody has already decided not to buy. We actually get a 12 percent increase in revenue with a downsell, so it's important to do. Most offline businesses have never even thought about a downsell.

We set up a fan page to start the sales process. We can build individual pages for the entire sales process on a separate website and then set up split testing. This allows us to know what's working and what isn't. We can have two different pages or two different pieces of content, two different offers, and test which one works the best, A versus B. Make sure you test your sales process. We test all of our links, our upsells, our downsells. We check our credit card processing. Make sure that your credit card processing is working and make sure you get paid, which is very important.

For just a simple sales process you can just embed a buy button on your Facebook page and take action takers right to check out. Of course, later you will want to send follow up emails from your autoresponder email system to continue to market offers to your new clients.

Traffic

Traffic is where it takes a little more time and effort. Frankly, we can have everything else right and if we don't have the traffic right we won't make any money. There are some paid methods, like pay-per-click, where we pay Google for each time someone clicks and they come to our page. There are also Facebook ads where you can specifically market to Facebook users based on several factors, including age, interests, location and more.

There are free methods like search engine optimization. SEO is very important because we want our pages to rank without effort except what we put in up front.

The Internet is a big place, but we can make fan pages from small sub-niches and drive traffic by focusing our keywords. When we do this correctly, we can literally dominate a certain niche on all those pages. It's all for driving traffic to get an opt-in and make sales.

Copywriting for getting fans to take action

The fan page title is the subject line and it's what captures people's attention or not. We create curiosity, we promise a benefit that speaks to the reader's interest. We want to get the person to continue reading, then make an unbelievable offer that they will find irresistible. This can either be a free giveaway to get their email address or a great product for sale. We want to help the reader to relate to whatever it is to keep them reading. Start with problems you have faced and end with a solution that you're offering.

If you want to sell a product from your fan page, then we recommend you educate your audience, which is the foundation of all good marketing, with information that the reader is interested in and why your product or services are the best. We want to include testimonials because social proof is a huge influencer. Video testimonials are most compelling because we can believe facial expressions and voice. Include a combination of video, photographs and text.

The Social Engine

Put that all together with Twitter and tweet to your followers to come to your page. We can also create short YouTube videos and then in those YouTube videos we can have a call to action at the end of them to go to your page.

It's amazing, the technology out there that in an offline business we just never had. On the Internet we can determine very quickly why something is down, why revenue is down, why this product isn't selling as well. We can make a quick change and see if we can pick it up again by changing the copy, call to action, offer or adding more to it for value.

Cydney's Social Wealth Action Steps:

1. If you don't already have Facebook, set an account up.
2. If you already have custom fan pages installed, spend time ensuring your default landing page is set up, your opt-in is embedded and look at it as if you were a new fan to make sure it's all engaging and easy to use. You can split tests on key components on multiple fan pages to improve the effectiveness of your pages.
3. Check all of your existing websites to ensure that they have analytics tracking installed so you can evaluate your advertising and traffic results and improve on them.
4. Do you have a product to sell now? If not, create one or visit Clickbank.com to find good products you can promote.
5. Do a copy review of your offer that one of your team members has prepared. Remember, offers must be relevant, compelling, have clarity of value, urgency and a clear call to action.

SECTION TWO

BUILD

If you make customers unhappy in the physical world, they might each tell 6 friends. If you make customers unhappy on the Internet, they can each tell 6,000 friends. If you do build a great experience, customers tell each other about that. Word of mouth is very powerful.

– **Jeff Bezos,** *CEO of Amazon.com*

CHAPTER 8

SET UP YOUR MILLIONAIRE SYSTEM

Brittany Lynch

'The Adwords Insider'

Brittany Lynch is an established online marketing expert specializing in paid traffic generation. As an account strategist for Google, she worked with Fortune 50 companies optimizing their search marketing campaigns to achieve the best return on investment possible. This experience has given her a unique advantage and insight into Google AdWords and other online paid traffic platforms. She now dedicates her time to teaching other entrepreneurs and small business owners her successful online marketing strategies.

Google as a powerful advertising medium

Making money and building business online creates so much opportunity to have flexibility in your life. To travel while working and just live life to the fullest, as well as earning an income, has been really nice for me.

I started making money online when I was 16. I went to my dad one day and wanted some money. He was involved with a soccer company at the time and had all these extra soccer DVDs. He said, "If you want some money, then you're going to have to work for it. If you want to make some money, you can sell these DVDs and you can get a 50 percent commission."

Going door-to-door didn't appeal to me, so my dad introduced me to the idea of AdWords, Google's pay-per-click program. I started building my first ad campaign online bidding on keywords related to soccer and trying to sell those soccer DVDs through the Internet. I had some success; that was my first project.

I was recruited out of university by Google, which was really exciting. I worked for Google from 2008 to 2009. I had the opportunity to stay on and extend my contract, but decided to pursue my own business. I started by selling my services building ad campaigns for small to mid-size businesses. After a while, I had replaced my income, but was still working long hours. So I decided products are definitely the way to go, not services. When you're in the service industry you are selling your time and I've learned that time is the one commodity you cannot get back.

When you're in the service industry you are selling your time and I've learned that time is the one commodity you cannot get back.

I transitioned my knowledge into products, using AdWords and paid traffic. I started sending this paid traffic to my web properties (my sales and opt-in pages), to build a mailing list and community. I have a mailing list and it's an asset; I will promote other people's products if they're the right fit, but I primarily promote my own. It takes only a few hours, depending on the scope, to make products. You get 100 percent commission and it helps build your brand and your authority, rather than someone else's. Now I have a million-dollar-a-year information marketing business and I couldn't be happier.

Promotions

Primarily I use online promotion, AdWords and Facebook advertising. I'll do a lot of media buys, buy traffic and send this to my squeeze pages to build my mailing list.

A media buy offline would be when you're buying a TV spot, a place in a magazine or an advertisement in a newspaper. Online it's very similar. If you imagine all of the billions of websites there are out there, a lot of them have ad space. It's actually going to that website and saying, "Hi, I'd like to place my ad on your website. How much is that going to cost?" That's a media buy.

I believe in paid traffic, it's so quick and instant; you can get traffic in as little as an hour. You can scale up infinitely. You can use it successfully as long as you know your numbers, how much your visitor is worth to you. I'm very good at driving paid traffic and getting a return on my investment.

I always tell people that there is no such thing as free traffic online. If you think of search engine optimization, there's time that goes into building those back links, writing those articles, building that immense amount of content to get traffic back to your site. It's not reliable and it's not all that scalable. Think of your opportunity cost.

I do from time to time send the people on my mailing list offline sales presentations or newsletters and that sort of thing. That has worked out really effectively as well, but online I find has the lowest barrier to entry and is the easiest and the most effective.

Management tools

I recently discovered Podio. It's like a Facebook for CRM or project management. You can plug in different apps, depending on the type of business you have. It's great for managing tasks, communicating between members, setting deadlines, creating projects.

It's hard to maintain a connection with tens of thousands of people. That's why I find webinars so useful. Everyone can get on, ask questions. It's an awesome way to maintain that community.

I use GoToWebinar to run my webinars. Skype is a low-cost way to maintain communication. I use PayPal to process my payments. I use ScreenFlow to record a lot of my videos. That's a great service.

As soon as you start your business or start hiring, it's important to start documenting your training. That's something I learned the hard way. Record videos of you going through the things that you do every day, record PDFs of your day-to-day tasks. When you do hire someone, you can pass that knowledge base along to them instead of doing it one-on-one.

When you've got a community that's tens of thousands of people, it's hard to maintain that connection with each member. That's why I find webinars so useful. Everyone can get on, ask questions. It's an awesome way to maintain that community.

Where do I begin?

It all starts with having an idea for a business or choosing a niche. I tell people, "Sit down, brain storm a list of things that you're passionate about and things that you're an expert on. Then use that as a basis for building a business." I'm a firm believer in information marketing as a business.

You can profit from passion. That's what is going to get you up every morning. Building your own business can be a challenge and there are obstacles. Find something you're passionate about and find a way to monetize around that. I also say that you can make a lot more money with a 'super niche' which is a topic that lots of people are passionate about and regularly spend money on.

> You can profit from passion. Find something you're passionate about and find a way to monetize that. That's what is going to get you up every morning.

Malcolm Gladwell says it takes about 10,000 hours to become an expert on something. I always set aside an hour a day to read. Find people that you've identified as successful and who align with your goals and follow them and the material that they release.

Ingredients for success

Number one, you really do need to know your goals. Be as specific as possible. If it's to make $10,000, make it by a specific date. Make your goal as firm as possible.

Number two is reverse-engineer your goals. If it's to make $10,000 in 30 days, how are you going to do that? Every day I sit down and write down the ten goals, short-term and long-term, that I want to achieve. Then beside those goals I work backwards. I say, "How do I achieve this goal?" Whether that goal is "Make $1,000 today" or "Run a marathon," how do I work backwards from that? If I want to make $10,000 this month, how many $50 products do I need to sell? I have to sell 200 x $50 products to make $10,000. Okay, so how many people do I need to add on to my mailing list in order to get them to purchase that many products?

I always start with the end in mind and then work backwards. That has worked really well for me. It makes you realize that nothing is impossible. Has someone made a million dollars a month before? Absolutely. What are they doing to make that million dollars a month? Make a plan for success.

Number three is "Persistence Beats Resistance". I think that's my favorite saying. Keep persisting, keep working towards your goal. You're going to run into obstacles. But if you keep persisting, you're going to reach your goals. That's the motto that I live by.

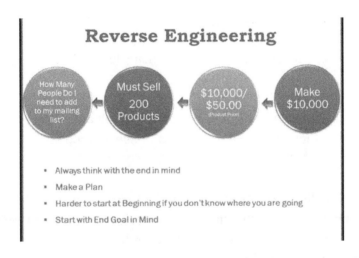

Strategy

Number one, you need traffic. You're always going to need traffic in an Internet business. You're going to need web property, so you're going to need a squeeze page; I often build my squeeze page right on Facebook, and ideally your own product. You can use other people's products, but I always aim to create my own. I have systems to help me create information products quickly.

Everything I do in my business is as systemized and automated as possible. Choose your traffic sources. Is it going to be AdWords or Facebook advertising or SEO? Is it going to be media buys? Pick one, work on that, become an expert, then move on to your second traffic form.

The second thing you need is something to sell. Are you going to create your own product or sell other people's? If you can find popular products to sell on Clickbank that is a good sign that there's a market in your niche.

Then I send traffic to my squeeze page to build my mailing list first. Send the traffic to a squeeze page rather than a sales page where you're going to lose most of your prospective customers. I think your mailing list is an asset.

As soon as people are on your mailing list, follow up with an email series. I have a very specific formula. I've got twelve emails that I use every time I go into a brand new niche, to build trust, establish my story and sell them my products. Then continue to build that relationship with them through email marketing and through webinars. I've got a formula for all that – a formula for choosing my niche, for setting up a squeeze page that profits well, a formula for my emails.

That's a short version of my millionaire secrets formula: establish traffic, get something to sell and make it into a system that you can rinse and repeat.

Establish traffic, get something to sell and make
it into a system that you can rinse and repeat.

I think building a Facebook profile and a Facebook fan page is important. I've got several fan pages. Building a fan page is essentially like a website but on Facebook, then with your fan page you can have an opt-in page on it. It's much like a community there, because people will "like" your fan page. You can ask your community questions, share your product links and share high value information relevant to them. You can even run and promote webinars on Facebook.

I use Facebook advertising to drive traffic to my fan page. You'll find if you target properly, about 80 percent of people will "like" your fan page. Not all of them will opt in to your mailing list, but having them on your fan page is like having a mailing list because you can build that community. It's the second best option. My fan page is www.facebook.com/brittlynch.

Pick a topic, and set up your success system and stay focused until you get it working. We're here to show you how to set it all up, you're not on your own.

Cydney's Social Wealth Action Steps:

1. Set up your professional Facebook page. For instructions and recommended resource providers who can set up highly effective and professional pages, visit www.MillionairesAcademy.com/Resources and look for "Facebook Solutions." Check out Brittany's Fan page.

2. Set up your professional YouTube profile and account, then record one short video per day with valuable information for your ideal prospects. After a few videos, you could post one per week. Facebook and Facebook users love videos and pictures as posts.

3. Conduct keyword research using Google's keyword tool to find hot topics in your niche and high search, low competition search terms. Brittany also suggests checking your topic in www.Dummies.com. They research the topics for their books very thoroughly.

4. Place a Facebook ad to promote your business page, but keep your budget low while learning to use the platform. I set a budget of $10 a day and did brilliant market research for this very book spending only $40 a week to get the information required to make essential marketing decisions.

5. Open your webinar account. At time of printing we use Gotowebinar, but for our latest recommended resources, visit the website at www.MillionairesAcademy.com/Resources .

CHAPTER 9

WEBINARS: CREATE, PROMOTE, SUCCEED!

Steven Essa

CEO, X10Effect

Steven Essa has emerged as a leading world authority on webinar marketing and online business. In less than two years, he's built a global client base and become a high profile speaker in New Zealand, the U.K., the U.S., Ireland and Australia. Steven has trained thousands of people to do what he does: create a dream life using the Internet. He has generated $4000, $8000 and even $25,000 in a single hour and makes it his mission to help others do the same.

My magic formula

Webinar is short for web-based seminar. It's like a seminar done on the Internet. You can use it to train people, to sell, to pitch things. Why webinars? They're cheap to run. For about $99 a month you can do webinars every single day, every hour. People also love webinars; they love learning from home. There's no headache for them, just turn on their computer and they can leave at any time they want, but they're the highest-targeted person at that time you could possibly be speaking to.

Unlike face-to-face selling, unlike phone selling, where normally it involves you springing up on the business owner and imposing your time on them, you've got them coming to you, which is the single biggest difference. That's the power.

If you can get somebody coming to a webinar with you, then they want to know about what you've got. That makes them the most highly-targeted prospect or customer at that given time.

It's huge value to you as well. It creates products for you! You can record webinars and use them over and over. It creates products on demand and builds you a huge mailing list. If you don't know yet–and most business owners in the offline world don't–the money is in the list, the mailing list of prospects and customers that have bought from you before. You can capture these names through a webinar and resell to those people many different products and services. You'll build a huge list if you apply webinars to your business.

Webinars also convert better than websites. You're looking to pick up a one percent conversion for a person coming to a website for the first time, if you're lucky. A good webinar will pick up a minimum of 10 percent conversion. Basically, the reason is that they can hear you. They can see that you know what you're talking about. The trust factor, the confidence factor in what you're doing is a lot higher with a webinar as opposed to a static website or a website with a video, a photo. With these statistics, if we have a $100 product and 100 people go to our website and 100 people go to the webinar, the website will sell one product for $100. The webinar will convert $1,000 worth of sales.

So here's my seven-step program for using webinars:

Step 1: Choose a webinar platform

There are a lot of different systems out there and webinars have been around for years, but only in the last few years has it become affordable to everybody. The system I use is GoToWebinar because it's the easiest one.

Once I've done a live webinar, I record it and I automate the process. We have a webinar replay system–"The Webinator"–that will play the webinar on autopilot. I can program the webinar and say "play this video at 9:00pm everyday" or "on Mondays." I can set the time in multiple time zones. Whenever someone joins your database, instead of sending them an email and then another and another and them waiting to see you and hear from you, you can have them go straight to an automated webinar.

The first email will say: "Congratulations on joining our list! We've got a webinar tonight all about exactly what you've joined our list to get." That means that you're delivering huge content, huge value and your opportunity to make the sale instantly has increased amazingly.

Step 2: Your webinar model

Now choose what webinar model to do. What are we going to deliver on the webinar? I've got it cut down to four main models:

    a. Show-and-tell
    b. Interview-an-expert
    c. Paid-up-front
    d. Joint venture

I use all four of these in my business, but I suggest if you're just getting started to choose one model for your first webinar and do that.

A show-and-tell webinar model is showing and telling about a product, service, or a concept that you've got.

What's great about the interview-an-expert model is that you don't have to be the expert in anything. Is Oprah Winfrey an expert? She's an expert at interviewing people now and she's become a billionaire as a result of it. You're asking questions and just sitting back and listening. You don't have to talk much when someone is passionate about what they're talking about. There's no shortage of experts out on the market with books, products and knowledge.

The paid-up-front model simply means that people pay before they get access. Instead of doing the webinar for free, you put a little webpage together or send out an email to everyone and say, "I'm doing a webinar on this particular topic. It's $50. You can click on this link and buy now and you can come."

The final one, joint venturing, is the best way you can make money because you can access other people's databases who have already built trust, who have already built up their credibility and their market. You can joint venture with them.

Step 3: Promote the webinar

What now? You can send an email to your list. I also do videos. One of the things I do in my live demonstrations, in my webinar seminar, is actually grabbing someone out of the audience and I interview them with a little flip camera. Do a couple of those videos, put them on YouTube, put the link underneath them and put them on your website. Video is a great way to promote.

You can do blog posts. Go to your website and put a blog post on: "Hey, guys, this week on the webinar, we're going to be doing an interview with Bruce. Click on this audio interview to listen to it or watch this video, or just click on this link and register for the webinar."

You could do joint ventures. You go to other people and say, "Hey, can you come and sell your product and service on my webinar?" Basically, "Can you come to my webinar and sell your stuff? I'll promote it." Or you go to other people and say, "Can you promote this webinar for me? I'll give you a commission off all the sales." Whatever it is that your margin is, you give it to them and they will email it for you. This is a very powerful way to generate a huge list by joint ventures. Other people promote for you, and you promote for other people and you make good money.

You can put your webinar link on Twitter, Facebook, YouTube, LinkedIn, Google+ and all the other social networks that are out there. Social media is a fantastic platform because even while I'm interviewing someone on a webinar, I go to Twitter and type in, "Hey, I'm on a webinar right now with Bruce talking about business cash flow" and put the link there. I find people joining my webinars even half-an-hour in. Once you get a name and email, straightaway they're in your funnel. They can hear you. Interview good experts, get good content, then you'll have a member for life.

Once you get a name and email, straightaway they're
in your funnel. Interview good experts, get good
content, then you'll have a member for life.

Write articles; I found you could actually get a very high SEO ranking from articles and article syndication. If you have someone writing articles for you, at the bottom you can say, "Hey, join Steven Essa for a weekly webinar at BigFatMarketing.com" or whatever it is for you.

You can use pay-per-click marketing. If you don't know what PPC marketing is, it's just like advertising in the paper, except you're doing it online and you only pay when someone clicks on your ad. Wouldn't that be good if the Yellow Pages were like that? PPC marketing means you can pay 30 cents, 40 cents, a dollar; it depends on how competitive your market is. On Google, Facebook,

Bing and all the other search engines, advertise; send people to your webpage and invite them straight to a webinar that night using the Webinator or whatever tool you're using.

If you're promoting via Facebook, set up an event for your webinar. If you're going to do an event, you can select your groups of people to invite. On Facebook, you might have friends in multiple markets. Do what we do and segment the list. Wherever we add a new friend, we put them into categories: Internet marketing, real estate, etc. Are they a relative? A friend? An Internet marketer? An acquaintance?

There are many ways to promote. I use one funnel at a time. I focus on joint venture, blog posts, videos, emails, social media. Focus on "What's the best and highest use of your time?" as Jay Abraham says. It's going to bring maximum results for minimal effort.

Step 4: Run the webinar

People say to me, "Isn't a webinar just the same as doing a video?" Definitely not. Have you ever tried having someone hold a camera in front of you and then they say, "Talk?" Then you turn into an idiot and you go, "Um, ahh… blah, blah, ehh…" You know so much about your market and your topic but you can't talk because a video is very intrusive, very scary. A webinar is like talking on the phone. You can talk like you're talking to one person, and you're in your room and no one can see you. You might be in pajamas; you're comfortable.

Normally, at around 5 to 10 minutes, you're going to lose people with video. With a webinar, you can put it into a step-by-step system, a presentation that people can follow. When people can follow you, learn step-by-step and see the method, and they're not looking at your face, they're looking at the screen and learning, then they're going to pay attention to what you're teaching more. You've got more chance of getting your message across and making a sale at the end. It's much more powerful than video.

There are some systems that allow you to ask questions, but let's say your system doesn't allow you to. The next day, in this auto-responder, Bob gets another email that says, "Hey, Bob! Did you make it to the webinar? What?!? You didn't make it? Well, here's the link again. If you did, that's great, excellent! What questions do you have for us?"

I've done webinars live. We generated $17,000 and then we sent out a replay and generated another $8000. I've got a student who generated

£17,000 on her first webinar, sent out an email nine days later, did it again and ran another £9,500. Another student did a real estate webinar and did £4,200 on the first webinar, and then sent out the replay and did another £1,800 in sales. The replay webinars produce a high conversion as well. Live or not live; it doesn't matter. Get it out there. Record it once and then automate it and send it out.

> Record your webinar once and then automate it
> and send it out. Live or not live; it doesn't matter.

Step 5: Collect the money

The simplest way to collect money online is PayPal. They charge about two percent. Sometimes with PayPal, if you make a lot of sales on a webinar ($20,000 to $50,000 or more) in a very short amount of time, PayPal gets scared because they think there's fraud going on. This has happened to me and a lot of friends. Here you are trying to run a business. You finally crack the code. You run a webinar and all of a sudden, you get shut down for doing the right thing. Well, that's just going to happen sometimes. Make sure you phone PayPal before your webinar and say, "We're doing a webinar, we could be collecting $10,000 to $50,000 or more. Don't freak out. I'm just letting you know now." That can help you tremendously and avoid them freezing your account while they investigate it.

If you want to collect money with your merchant account online, then you go to your bank and say, "I want a merchant account to process money online," and they'll give you the information you need to fill in. It normally takes about three weeks to do that.

You can also put your products on ClickBank and they collect the money for you. You could have a replay webinar on a ClickBank page.

Accelerated wealth secret:
Step 6: Automate the webinar

Put all of your webinar replays into auto-responder sequences. When someone joins your database for real estate, the first video you send out is a webinar on, for example, how to research the market.

The first video you send out is why they joined. If on your website you said, "Join my website and I'll show you this," then run a webinar on that and offer it to them straightaway. It's automatic. You don't have to pre-program it; it's done, which means you do the work once and you get paid over and over again for people coming through.

If you're not converting one in ten, (that means for every ten people who join your database, if you're not converting one of those into a sale), then there's something wrong with your webinar. It's normally one of two things. The first thing is what you offered was not irresistible. Always try and make what you're offering an absolutely irresistible offer, a bargain offer that's really, really good value for them. It doesn't have to be cheap, but it has to be huge value stacked in their favor. Normally, I gauge that by my stomach. When I set the price for something, if I go, "Ooh, I'm ripping myself off on this one," that's normally a good sign that your offer is irresistible. They you have more confidence to sell it that way as well.

Always make an absolutely irresistible offer. It doesn't have to be cheap, but it has to be huge value stacked in their favor.

The second reason why you wouldn't be making money from a webinar is more than likely that what you presented, the content, didn't match what you were selling at the end. For example, if you were talking about real estate, talking about how to do lease options, and in the presentation you're saying, "This is how you buy a property with no money doing a lease option." Then at the end you try to sell them a house and they need a deposit. It doesn't make sense because you just told us how to do it for free and now you're trying to sell me a house where I need a deposit. There's a disconnect. I call it mish-mash; it's a mismatch.

So just remember, make an irresistible offer and don't mish-mash! Make sure your presentation and the offer make sense together. You'll be surprised how many times I'm watching a webinar and I'm going, "Oh my god. They're leaving so much money on the table! That's so confusing." Make sure you don't have that same problem when you run your webinars.

Accelerated wealth secret:
Step 7: Affiliates

Affiliates are people who love your product and want to sell it. They tell people about it. Anyone who talks about your product or service to anybody else is an affiliate. What you can do for your affiliates is reward them by giving them a commission and say to them, "Anyone who turns someone into a sale is going to get a commission from us."

Give them the tools, too. If you've written an email already that works, give them that. You say, "Hey, Mr. Affiliate, here's an email that you can send out to your list. Here's the special affiliate link that you put there so we can track sales back to you. Here are the banners that we've used. We've already written the email and it's already signatured from you as well. Here are the things that we've written on Twitter, the things we've put on Facebook that work." This is where most people go wrong. Give your affiliates the tools and the resources and say, "Here you go and if you need anything else, let us know and we'll create it for you." That affiliate is going to send it out and you're going to make money from that.

You can even have the affiliate record the voiceover for the start and end of the webinar, if you want it to sound believable, like they were there, so their database believes in it more. You can have them record the intro. You send them a script that says, "Hi, everyone, welcome to the webinar! Today we're going to talk to Steven Essa and he's going to tell you all about webinars." Then at the end, you have another script. He says, "Wow, that was great, Steve! Now go and take that offer." You edit the voice at the start and at the end of your webinar, and it sounds like they're on the webinar with you. If he's mailing it out to his list, it sounds like he's there and that builds credibility. Affiliates mean higher conversions and free traffic.

Affiliates mean higher conversions and free traffic.

It's going to cost you a lot more money and a lot more time to go and build a list of 10,000 people that you can email your webinar to, than if you went to somebody who's already got 10,000 in that market and said, "Hey, can I give you x percent for any sales you make when you mail this webinar out to your subscribers? I've tested it and it's converting one in ten, two in ten in some cases." You just tell them what the statistic is. Be honest, because you'll get called out; they'll mail it and they'll never mail again. Test it out first.

Don't try and build the list yourself. It will cost you more and take more time. Go to these people and email it to their list and give them a commission. That, my friends, is how you build a multimillion-dollar business using webinars. That's the millionaire secret, instead of trying to do it all yourself!

Cydney's Social Wealth Action steps:

1. Choose which model of webinar you will run: paid or free, educational, joint venture or interview.
2. Prepare an informative, hot-topic presentation to run via webinar for your existing database using PowerPoint or similar presentation software. The webinar can be from 20 minutes to 2 hours long, depending on the value and complexity of your topic.
3. Send out invitations, at least two weeks prior, with a reminder the day before, to attend the webinar. Use email, Facebook events, LinkedIn reminders and Twitter posts to spread the word. Video emails can also be very effective.
4. Set up a survey to collect feedback from your attendees as soon as they are finished your webinar.
5. Invite your colleagues and database to become affiliates and promote your webinars as services for their clients and customers. Discuss joint venture opportunities, sponsorships, future interviews and other opportunities where you and your colleagues mutually benefit.

CHAPTER 10

CONTINUITY INCOME SYSTEMS

Alicia Lyttle

CEO, Monetized Marketing LLC

Alicia Lyttle is an author, speaker and CEO of My Golden Rolodex. Since leaving her job ten years ago as an Environmental Justice Specialist in the White House, Alicia has helped thousands around the world learn the power of the Internet. Together with her sister, Lorette, they have built over 250 websites and generated millions of dollars online over the last ten years. She is an expert in social networking, membership sites, affiliate marketing, outsourcing and so much more.

Alicia holds a Bachelor's Degree from Tulane University, a Master's Degree from the Tulane School of Public Health and Medicine and is currently working to complete her Ph.D. from the University of Michigan. Her true passion is working with people, creating strategies and systems to leverage the Internet to create financial success and personal freedom.

Create a residual income

Why do I teach about building continuity programs? It's because the power and the freedom that it allows entrepreneurs to have is immeasurable. You're not having to sell one e-book anymore, you're selling a membership. People now belong to a club – and you're getting paid month after month. All of us entrepreneurs want more stability and better growth. We would like to know how much is coming into our business every month. We would like to be able to grow, putting in new members, to grow our income.

So I'm going to talk about the five steps to massive membership site success. These are:

Step 1: Identify your passion

So, what do you love to do? What do others say that you're good at? What problem can you help solve for other people?

You can set up a residual program, or membership, for whatever you have. You just have to think outside the box and really set something up. You might think that you're unique, but somebody else out there is already doing it, so look at what other models are out there and how you can take that model and add to it.

So for those dog lovers out there, there is a dog treat of the month club. This is a company that's already making dog treats, and they're monetizing it by building in a monthly program for it. We also have a teddy bear of the month club. You get a new teddy bear each and every month. Those are some fun ones, but the clubs most of us are used to seeing are like the CD, newsletter or product of the month club. I just wanted to give you those examples, especially for offline retail businesses.

So now we're going to look at digital products for residual income and some models. The first one is information-based membership sites. There are author-based membership sites. One of my favorite authors is David Bach who has a whole series called *Finish Rich* and a membership site based on the teachings in his books.

You could have a guru-based membership site, a membership site based around you and your teaching, where you're the expert. Or you could have a product-based club and charge per month to get training, resources and support for the product you're selling.

Step 2: Create a website

Take your passion and now monetize it. First, you need for your website a lead capture page (aka a squeeze page or opt-in page), somewhere you collect people's information because they are interested in what you have to offer. Then a sales page – you need testimonials, people you've worked with, your system processes or whatever you do that has worked well for them. You have their stories. You also need a way to collect money on time.

The basic funnel formula starts with a lead capture page. That lead capture page goes to a sales page and that sales page goes to your membership site. This is just a basic formula. You use your lead capture page to capture people's information. Then you use your sales page to take the sale and forward them into your membership site.

Start off with just the basics. Have future growth in mind: multiple landing pages, up sales, down sales, tie backs and that sort of stuff.

Register a domain name. You want your domain name to make sense and be keyword rich; make sure you have a domain name that is keyword rich and easy for people to remember.

Let's say you want to do a membership about training pit bull dogs and you know that people are searching for that exact phrase when they are typing into Google. If "pitbulltraining.com" is your domain name, when they type it in you're going to be the number one position or at least on the first page of Google for that word because those keywords are in your domain name.

The next thing is creating content. People make what we call private label rights products that you can "private-label." That is, you can put your name on it and sell it as if it's your own. It's a great way to create new content for your site without having to create it all yourself. It would be the same thing as hiring a writer, except when you hire a writer that content is usually yours and not shared with anybody. When you do it with private label rights, you don't know how many other people have that same content and have the rights to it as well. If you do buy private label rights, edit it and make it your own.

With private label rights, you have the right to re-label and change the content that you buy. Using the pit bull training, let's say somebody wrote a report on potty training a puppy. They say for $17 you can buy this report, put your name on it and change it in any way you like. That means you can re-label it as your own and sell it, put it in your site, give it away or do whatever you want with it.

One of the things that my sister and I have been doing recently is what we call it the "Plank Method" because we got it from our friend Robert Plank. He says if you can create content, why don't you take three days out of your life, lock yourself in a room, rent a room or a conference center and create content for three days you can load into you site.

The last step in getting a website is two things: an auto-responder so that you can automate the whole process and a membership site plugin. Wishlist is one plugin that allows you to make your WordPress site into a membership site. The auto-responder we use to tie everything together is iContact, to automate messages and everything going out.

Step 3: Automation

This is about removing yourself from the equation. You want to make sure that your systems work while you're sleeping. We call this the "set it and forget it model." Set everything up in your business and have the ability to walk away and forget it.

Having an Internet business, automation is just so important. We're talking about setting up automated emails, having registration be automated, your content release automated. So having the tools you need in your business to automate things are important.

Here are some examples of what you can do:

You can schedule your posts to go out on the day that you want them to go out. You could write all your content and load it and have it release over time. One of the things that we like to do as well is to have modules, released every seven days. If you have a course, release it over time. Show upcoming posts; it's nice if people can see what's coming up. We call this the stick strategy. People want what they can't have. So imagine in your membership someone is thinking "I don't know if I'm going to pay next month, I'm getting a lot of value, but I just don't know." If they see what's coming up next, and it's content they want and they know if they're not a member, they're not going to get it. So they stick in because they see what's coming.

Show upcoming posts; it's nice if people can see
what's coming up because people want what they
can't have. We call this the stick strategy.

If you're creating a site, and you want to set it up for automation, y make sure you have the content to load in, so you can automate it. You can't automate what you don't have.

On a daily basis, you should have a forum where you can deliver a conversation with your members. It should have a community feel where your members login every day and maybe get rewarded for it. Every week you should do webinars and you could do videos that you send out or a newsletter. Every month you could give courses out, or articles, or interview experts. Then yearly–this is something that is great for higher-level memberships–you can do retreats, seminars or a mastermind meeting. These are just some examples, and what you deliver also depends on what you are charging for your membership.

If you're charging $7.95 a month, maybe they get one course a month, or one interview a month, or one newsletter. If you're charging $500 a month, maybe have everything on the list above.

Step 4: Traffic

Ways we drive traffic to our sites are by affiliates, social media, articles, video marketing, SEO, posting on forums, writing our blog and commenting on other people's blogs.

Here are some of these traffic strategies:

- Facebook: Build a Facebook fan page and you can put ads out on Facebook that cost a few pennies a click. You can have affordable ads, drive people to a Facebook fan page where they can opt in to find out more about you or receive something free. I encourage you to look into that as a strategy for generating leads.
- YouTube: Did you know that YouTube is the second largest search engine? People go to Google to find stuff, but they also go to YouTube. Create videos with free content that lead back to your offer.
- Articles: Write articles! When people are searching and you have an article written on that topic with keywords in it, people find your articles. At the bottom of your article put your contact information and how people can find out more.
- Twitter: Every time I send out a tweet, I drive traffic to whatever I'm promoting, so I am using Twitter to promote different products and services and keep in touch. Twitter is powerful for driving traffic to a blog.
- Blogs: Blogs are important because you can take all of the content that we've talked about – writing articles, tweets, YouTube videos – and put

them on your blog and drive traffic to your blog, which has an ad for your offer.

- Forums: These are where people chat about specific topics. Let's say you want to find people talking about dog training. In Google, you would type in "dog training forum" or "dog training discussion board" and you would find forums and discussion boards of people talking about your subject. If you're part of conversations on your subject, that will definitely help you to be able to recommend your product or services to the people that are discussing those topics.

Accelerated wealth secret
Step 5: Outsourcing

With outsourcing you can build a team of experts, have others create content for you, have others build your website or do anything that you don't want to do yourself. We have people in the Philippines, which is where the largest part of our team comes from, Malaysia, Pakistan, Jamaica and Romania. Our team is from all across the world.

What can you hire an assistant do for you? What can you outsource? Social networking, Facebook fan pages, Twitter, article marketing, video marketing, blogs, social book marking, back linking, researching, telemarketing, customer support, database, and much, much more.

Communicate with your team and if you're training them, train with video. If you train them with video and you need to replace that person, or bring someone else on to do that job, you have all the videos in your archive. You can send the new person to the video training. You shouldn't do one-on-one training or over the phone. Do videos or a webinar.

Communicate with your team and if
you're training them, train with video.

Require the person who is working with you to report to you daily, weekly, whatever you feel comfortable with and whatever method you feel is best for recording. I find that helps to eliminate a lot of questions. You don't have to say, "What did you do today? Where is this project?" Tell them to tell you what they've done, where the projects are at and what they need from you. Have the communication program in place so it's as pleasant an experience for you as possible. At the beginning of every week ask them to send you a report called a "looking ahead" report: what's up for this week, what are they working on this week, if they need more to work on.

My next suggestion when outsourcing is to write up a plan. So what is your plan? What are your goals? What's the media you are going to use to deliver your plan? Who is going to work on it? What are the tasks they are going to do?

Let's look at one: the goal is to build relationships with clients. You want to do that on your Twitter and Facebook pages. You want your virtual assistant, Julie, to do it. So what you say is, "Julie, send out one tweet a day and one Facebook post a day, and I want you to do some outreach. Reply to everyone who has sent a comment."

You need to outline your plan. What do you want your staff to do? How do you want them to do it? What are the tasks they're supposed to do, and who is going to be getting it done? It's important in defining that even before you hire someone. Really think about how you can structure your business to make it work better for you.

Cydney's Social Wealth Action Steps:

1. Review your business revenue model. Does your current model require you to sell over and over to new clients, or is it predominantly structured to foster ongoing relationships and sales with your existing and future client base?

2. What could you do to further encourage ongoing relationships with your clients?

3. What are your competitors doing? What are other businesses outside of your industry doing? Could you modify their systems to suit your industry?

4. How many of your business systems are automated? Allocate a member of your team to review your system automation from the customer experience perspective as well as from the perspective of those who manage the systems.

5. Do some brainstorming: what can you systemize immediately that will improve your customer conversions now?

CHAPTER 11

LEVERAGE THROUGH CELEBRITY ALLIANCES

Greg Writer

Founder and CEO, Children's
Educational Network Inc.

Greg Writer is the CEO and Founder of Children's Educational Network Inc., Angel Network.com and Club Tuki. He has over 28 years of experience in corporate finance, capital formation, executive level management, mergers, acquisitions, software development and sales and marketing. At the age of 21, he was the youngest owner of a full service investment bank in the United States, where he was involved in the financing of hundreds of small early stage startup companies. He is also a nationally known professional speaker, trainer and coach in the areas of marketing online and offline as well as child safety online. He currently owns and operates over 30 money-making websites that have approximately 1 million visitors every month.

Don't miss the boat!

I was born into a very, very wealthy family. My dad was a multimillionaire, my granddad was a multimillionaire. My uncles are multi-millionaires and if anyone is from Denver, Colorado, well, in downtown Denver amongst all of the high rises there is a whole square block named after my family. I was very fortunate.

Then, my parents got divorced when I was three. I went to live with my mom and visited my dad. The best way to describe my childhood is when I went out to dinner with my mom and stepdad, the bill was maybe $80. When I went to visit my father and went out to dinner, the *tip* was $200.

When I was 19, I dropped out of college. I went to visit my dad and he had just bought this brand new Jaguar XJ-12. I got into the front seat with him and he had a big stack of stock confirmations in the front seat. He was on his way to the accountant. I asked, "What are these?"

He said, "Those are my tax receipts from all of the stocks that I have been trading."

I asked, "Stocks? What are stocks?" He started telling me that he made a lot of money in the stock market. I said, "How much money?"

And he said, "Oh, about $5 million!"

I'm like, "$5 million?!?! Wow! I want to learn the stock market!"

And he said, "Well, I'll teach you. Do you have any money saved up?" I had been pounding nails working construction and I had $2,000 saved up. He got my $2,000 into a stock where I bought 20,000 shares of stock at 10 cents a share, and I ended up selling that stock in about four months at 70 cents a share. I had turned my $2,000 into $14,000. I'm like, "I have found my home!! I want to be a stock magnate; I want to invest."

The first thing that I want to share is that opportunities come along and when you don't take advantage of them you really have a chance of missing the boat. It's about relationships; the reason my father got this is because he was wealthy and the wealthy work with the wealthy. The "good ol' boy" network was in place, and because he was in that network, I got a piggyback on a deal. They're not going to invite an average guy to put $2,000 in a hot deal, right? My dad put in $100,000 and I piggybacked to off of his $100,000 and ended up making 2100 percent on my money. Did anyone invite you to invest in Google? Did you get invited to invest in Microsoft back when they went public? Do you know who got invited to invest in Google? Tiger Woods.

So that was the world I got into and I ended up getting my securities license and becoming an investment banker. We had a lot of successes, but for every one of those successes there were 10 losers. So I don't want anyone to think that I was just like the golden guy who everything I touched turned to gold. No, we raised money and took risks on a lot of deals. I'm a risk taker. I liked the excitement that was associated with it. After 20 years I can say there are ways to minimize your risk by knowing what you're doing. I believe that if you're not learning you're dying, you're going backward. The only thing between people getting what they have and what they want in life is knowledge.

If you're not learning you're dying, you're going backward.
The only thing between people getting what they have
and what they want out of life is knowledge.

When you lose millions of dollars investing in companies that go out of business, you start to figure what didn't work. Almost all of the time it boils down to two components, literally like 98 percent of the time companies fail for these two reasons, management and marketing.

The Joy of Club Tuki

Today my passion is about doing something meaningful for children; that's what Club Tuki is all about. My daughter stumbled across a pornographic website, so that got me into looking at parental control software. TUKI is the acronym for "The Ultimate Kids' Internet." I got completely passionate about this and I wanted to create the world's largest online network for kids to protect and educate them.

I also wanted to educate them in the area of financial literacy, child obesity and success principles because these things are just not taught. Self-esteem and bullying are huge issues for which we can utilize this medium of the Internet to make a difference in the lives of kids.

So what we did that's different than anybody else on the Internet is we came to the conclusion that we need technology to protect, but we need education to teach.

I want children to learn by playing games. I want them to have fun while learning. I want them to be learning and not even know that they're learning. So we started to create games that taught Internet safety, technology responsibility, money and finance, nutrition, success principles and self-esteem.

Then my son came to me when he was about 12 or maybe 14. He said, "How are you going to get kids to play these stupid educational games?" So we ended up creating a very unique patented system where when children complete a game, they actually earn money. We call it "Tuki Moolah" and right now it correlates with U.S. currency, but my goal is to convert it for all around the world. So, no matter what part of the world you live in you earn this money that correlates to your currency. You can play a game and earn money.

Now this is the basis for teaching financial literacy because they have credits, debits and balances. Then what happens is they take this money and it goes into their own bank account. They learn about the debits and credits, and they can take this and go into an auction and bid and win real stuff. So they're being rewarded for playing educational games. I told my son when he wanted a $450 Nike driver (he's a golfer), "If I put a $450 Nike driver in the auction, then you could play educational games and win that driver. Then would you play those games?"

He said, "Yup, that would do it."

When YouTube came out we thought, we have to find the hot hungry market, we have to find out what they want and give it to them. We recognized that kids really like YouTube, but we can't let the kids go to YouTube because there is a lot of inappropriate, unsafe content on YouTube. So we created our own YouTube and we call it Tuki TV. All of the content is appropriate, child safe, G-rated.

Then we said if kids are going to use the Internet, they have to have an email account, so we created a complete kid-safe email system where they can only get emails that are approved by their parents. We've got this whole platform where the kids are playing games, earning money, winning real stuff, they have a safe email system and a safe YouTube system. Now our technology platform is so good that we private label it.

Accelerated wealth secret:
Private labeling

My most effective marketing method is my private labeling strategy. We can private label Club Tuki and all of our games, our auction, Tuki TV, the whole Club Tuki platform. We private label through a website called YourKidsClub. com. My strategy there is that I spent millions of dollars on my platform. Now we're going to help you brand it with your brand and then you're going to become our marketing and distribution partner. We'll supply technical support, customer support, and all of the technical stuff on the back-end and then we'll share in revenues together.

DreamWorks

Our deal with DreamWorks took me five months diligently knocking on doors, calling, and snail mailing to get into the door and get the meeting set up. I said I want to build the world's first Shrek Browser for kids and when kids use this browser your brand is always going to be on the desktop, no matter where you go your brand is always on the desktop. Even if they're watching your competitor's website, your brand is always on the desktop.

Your brand is the most valuable piece of real estate on planet Earth. I just hammered the brand, the brand, the brand, because I know that's what they're about. I did my research, I did my homework and they want that brand recognition. I delivered them a piece of technology that says, "Let's partner, I'll be the technology guy, we'll brand it with your brand and we'll share some revenues." So I got that deal.

Your brand is the most valuable piece of real estate on planet Earth.

Miss America

Same thing with Miss America; they wanted it for the branding. Miss America came out in 2007 and said her platform was Internet safety. She went around the country promoting our product and leveraging her name to get exposure for Internet safety. We got to ring the bell at NASDAQ and there in Times Square on the world's largest television screen they put our logo: Children's Education Network presents the Miss America Kid Safe Web Browser–and they left that up on the screen for three hours that day. I talked to the people at NASDAQ about that and they said it is $2,200 a minute to advertise on that screen.

Then we thought we have to get the next Hannah Montana. We're very fortunate that we got Cymphonique and we believe she will be as big a brand as Hannah Montana. She sings, acts and dances. She's got a show with Nickelodeon and a Sony distribution contract for her music. She has 27 million views on her Myspace page and her show hasn't even launched yet. Her music videos on YouTube have three or four million views already.

With her we did a partnership, a joint venture where we created the BYou–"Be Your Own You"–self-esteem clothing line, all about building self-esteem in girls, and she's our official spokesperson for Club Tuki. So you can see it on her site that gets lots of traffic and when her show launches on Nickelodeon she will probably get a million people a week to this website, probably a million people a day… and every single one of those will find out about Club Tuki.

So again, I have private labeled my technology for her and we cut the deal for her to promote us, be our spokesperson. She wants to use her fame and fortune to make a difference in lives of kids and we delivered that platform to her.

McGruff the Crime Dog wanted it for safety reasons. We leverage that same concept going, "Would you like to use our technology platform to extend your brand, offer your customers safety and education and build customer loyalty because you're helping protect and educate kids?" People don't say no to me very often because who says no to protecting and educating kids? It always makes them look good.

Social responsibility is good business

The social responsibly side of this is the socially responsible opportunity. Social media marketing is like a hot buzzword, but it's also where you seek to influence social behaviors, not necessarily to benefit me the marketer, but to benefit the target audience and the general society at large. I take that literally; I'm going to promote Internet safety, technology responsibility and online self-esteem.

I'm going to be an advocate for people to be responsible Internet users, with the intention that this is going to be good for the market at large. Now, if people want to come and buy my product after the fact, that's great! What happens is from a psychological standpoint I build credibility, I build rapport and I get brand recognition. Then, inevitably people are looking me up, they see what's attached to me and they go, "Wow, I'm going to go get that stuff from Greg because I love what he's all about. I love what he's doing."

So I don't have to go out there and hammer, "Buy my stuff, buy my stuff." I have hundreds of meetings and radio and television interviews. I get to say, "Whether you get my product or not, whether you get my tools or not, do something to protect your kids. Do something to be proactive about what's going on online."

It's really important that whatever your product or service is, you try to find what about it is socially responsible so it's meaningful and helpful to the market, to bring value as a whole. It's going to build credibility and pay off in the end – that's the whole law of reciprocity.

Accelerated wealth secret: Leverage strategic relationships

I'm really looking for those strategic relationships that you can leverage. I think that leverage is one of the key things that everybody should figure out how to do. I'm also one of these guys that believe you can get to anybody.

So here's my approach. I'll go into a business and start with, "Okay who are your top 100 dream clients?" If you could just get some of these dream clients your money would go through the roof. I could typically double or triple any businesses sales with this one strategy. I'm talking about your dream clients, just take the blinders off. If you could get that contract, who would it be? Then, I would get those top 100 and we start looking at them and narrow it down to the top 10. Then, if you can just get these top 10 you would blow it up, but if you get two of them, it would double or triple your business. Typically you can do that with almost any business, going okay with two or three of these dream clients you're going to double or triple my business, then, it's just about a marketing strategy and a tactical campaign to get to those people.

I tactically and strategically said I want to get DreamWorks. I want to get Shrek because that's like an anchor tenant. If I get Shrek and I get that deal, then I can get anything else. I've proven it over time. We've got Cymphonique, and I got Time magazine and Miss America, but I got Shrek first. And now, whenever I talk to anybody and I say I got Shrek, people who know who Shrek is – which is most people – go, "Wow!" That's instant credibility, so the sales cycle is shortened.

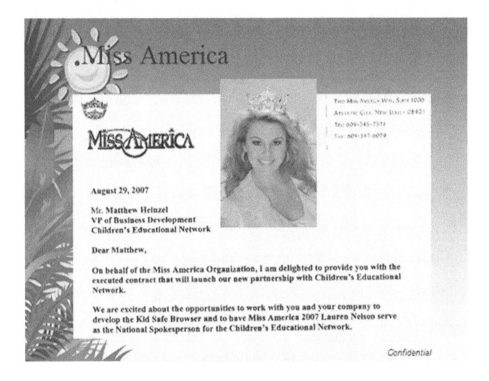

I leveraged Shrek and Miss America into Time, then Miss America and Time into McGruff and you just keep leveraging and leveraging these relationships until it gets you to where you want to go. You have to be strategic about that. You can't just get a list of these dream clients and go after them. You have to get the list, and then you have to do your research. You have to look them up and find out what they're hot buttons are, what are they about? Are they really the right strategic dream partnership?

You just keep leveraging and leveraging these relationships
until it gets you to where you want to go.

"Show me the money!"

I recently had a guy join my Board of Directors. His name is Lee Steinberg. He's the number one sports agent in the country; the movie *Jerry Maguire* was based on him. I was talking to him about wanting to private label my technology for the sports industry. So I wanted to get to the NFL and create, let's say, a San Diego Chargers kids' safe browser and a Dallas Cowboys kids' safe browser.

I said to him I also want to get to Phil Nicholson, the golfer. He said, "Don't spend your time going after Phil Nicholson because he doesn't have the reach or the distribution for kids that a football team would have." From his standpoint, strategically you don't spend energy going after Phil Nicholson if you can get the NFL. If I get the NFL, boom, you get all of these teams nationwide. Phil Nicholson is just one golfer.

Cydney's Social Wealth Action Steps:

1. Is your business supporting a meaningful cause? If so, have you explored opportunities to cross-promote in ways that can develop celebrity alliances for your business?

2. If your business benefits others, how could you be taking advantage of opportunities to promote the good work you do?

3. Organize a goodwill press campaign. Issue press releases and set up a social media blitz. You may be well served to engage a professional for this job, applying all the common sense principles of accountability, caution and budget management.

4. Review your sales model and product/service offering. Could it be adapted to a licensing or franchise model? Consider this: people are probably looking for an offering like yours to sell in their business. Other people may very well be willing to pay you to become your sales team.

5. Consider celebrity alliances to boost your brand and media appeal. To find out more about celebrity alliances, visit www. MillionairesAcademy.com/Alliances.

CHAPTER 12

SOCIAL B2B STRATEGIES

Sharon Williams

Founder and CEO, Taurus Marketing

Sharon Williams is the Founder and CEO of Taurus Marketing. Her professional experience includes management training with renowned U.K. retailer Marks & Spencer and various marketing management roles in the IT, shipping and travel industries. Her clients have included QBE Insurance, Kaz Computers and Napoleon Perdis. She is a councilor of the Australian British Chamber of Commerce and the American Chamber of Commerce: Women in Leadership Board. In addition, Sharon serves as an advisor for the University of Notre Dame, Chris O'Brien Lifehouse Ride to Conquer Cancer and the TransTasman Business Circle.

Be part of the dialogue

Media mogul Rupert Murdoch said in 2007, "A fundamental shift has occurred in marketing. *To find something comparable, you have to go back 500 years to the printing press, the birth of mass media—which, incidentally, is what really destroyed the old world of kings and aristocracies.* As a result of our changing world, technology is shifting power away from editors, the publishers, the establishment, the media elite." Away from brand managers and companies back to the consumers. The old marketing style was a monologue; the new digital marketing method is through dialogue, such as with Facebook pages where fans can voice their likes, or dislikes, of the brand directly to the brand managers or owners.

What we're hearing is we've got this new age of marketing, but I think we've had an ever-evolving age of marketing for the last 25 years. When I started out working for a wealthy shipping magnate, we had the ultimate in technology; our communication tool to half a million ton tankers around the globe was a telex machine! We got excited about the arrival of the fax machine and when the Internet arrived, we saw a whole new set of communication tools. Now, of course, we have social media. So, rather than a new age, I think it's an evolving age and the main exciting thing about this newer, or evolved, age is that instead of talking *at* people, we're talking *with* people.

Media communication means have changed over the years. I think in marketing we just have to be grown up about that. We have to make sure that we're on the ball and accepting every new medium as it comes, without panic, and embrace new things with cautious optimism and an open mind.

We have to make sure that we're on the ball and accepting of every new medium as it comes, without panic, and embrace things with optimism and an open mind.

Every so often I get a new tool to play with, in terms of being able to communicate. In 1995 we had the Internet hit. I remember my first DOS screen, then we had graphical user interfaces. We've had things like Second Life emerge and die and MySpace emerge and contract. There are lots of new things that come about, as much as we get excited about them, we look at them with an element of business caution as well as visualize the opportunities. The five Ps of marketing just don't exist anymore in their traditional sense.

Facebook, in terms of the people that belong, comes second only to India and China in size. Whether you like it or not, this is a new communication platform that has bulk and an unrivalled sense of belonging. With YouTube, we have the power of video to incorporate; indeed, YouTube is "the next big thing." . My children are already loading their own video content. Overnight sensations emerge like never before. You need to be carrying around your little Flip video and taking those 30-second video clips and going back and popping them up on the website really quickly.

Facebook, in terms of the people that belong,
comes second only to India and China in size.

Then we've got Twitter. Twitter and tweeting is all about being in connection with your customer by the minute, by the second, in 140 characters or less. That's great for dealing with customer problems, complaints or inquiries. It's great for breaking news stories. We saw in the recent earthquakes in Asia that we were getting the photos sent through to the newsrooms before the newsrooms could get their film cameras mobilized in the field.

I really think it's worth companies now getting video software in-house and the little Flip videos can make it really cheap. You don't have to go to the big corporate expense like we used to to make good productions.

We do have to be in the mindset that we're going to be having a conversation. We've got Facebook, YouTube, blogging, LinkedIn and Twitter. LinkedIn is your main tool for business-to-business communications. Everyone should be on LinkedIn. Your own personal brand and network is more important than ever, with stats saying the average individual will work for 12 different firms before they retire.

You've got to have a personal profile out there and make sure that it is appropriate. We've been talking about putting things on Facebook. Make sure that when someone looks for you, that digital resume that they see equates to who you really are. Make sure you control it. The message is to get engaged, but be cautious at the same time.

We really do have a whole new world of being able to communicate with people. One of the things we're doing is getting our entire customer database on LinkedIn. We're trying to get everybody on Facebook. We're extending the range of videos that we've got on YouTube.

Consumers check in before they buy

Ninety percent of Australians use social media to influence their purchasing decisions. Most people will think of something and then go check it out on the web or the social media sites to help determine what they're going to buy. The important thing is that this is absolutely affecting the way we buy and therefore should affect the way we sell. The sales landscape is changing and I think this is where it starts to hit home. Social media in the business world is so powerful. Social media communication can affect share prices and how businesses are operating. No more ivory towers for sales people, communication professionals and marketers everywhere.

> Social media is absolutely affecting the way we
> buy and therefore should affect the way we sell.

Facebook and Twitter alone account for a fifth of online traffic. We're spending more time, two-thirds more time on these sites than a year ago. This is where you need to be or someone else will be there taking your spot. Look at

Taurus Bullseye©

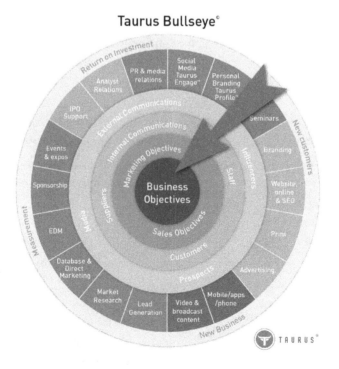

these figures: 1.5 million Australians on Twitter; Facebook, 9.2 million. We've only got 22 million in the country and almost half of them are on Facebook. YouTube, I said before, that's our future; it's the second most searched global network. If you're not up on YouTube, if haven't got a video, you're wasting an opportunity.

> If you're not up on YouTube, if you haven't
> got a video, you're wasting an opportunity.

The reality is, look, it's here now. It's happening now. It's not a case of doing it next year or the year after. By that point we'll have different media in place. It's a case of being on the ball and engaging with your customers; we talk about target markets, which is everybody: media, prospects, influencers and of course, your customers, and your staff and your potential staff. That's who you want to engage with; it's here now. We can start that today. If you haven't, you are already behind.

The other thing, of course, is that in terms of communications and running businesses, the world is talking. Are we listening? While we're not engaging on these platforms, our competitors will be. While we're not talking to people on those platforms, we're giving others a competitive edge. We need to be there. We've gone from sending advertising and PR messages out to engaging with audiences and being able to have a conversation. That's what social media has done for us. It's given us new tools to engage in conversations.

B2B social marketing

The B2B (business-to-business) industry is actually leading the way online, as opposed to the B2C (business-to-consumer) world. You'd think it was the other way around, wouldn't you? But 81 percent of B2B companies have got company-related profiles on social networks, compared to only 67 percent of B2C. The fact is that B2B selling is more about relationship building. Social media allows you to build a relationship in a better way than advertising, TV ads or being at an expo. Social media is immediate and it's a connecting thing. That's been very exciting in the B2B world to have these tools opposed to the more formal ways of marketing that we would all have been used to.

The B2B world is more targeted and focused because you know who you're going after. Social media has really changed the way B2B business is done and has been a great tool. The best tool you can have for a salesperson is LinkedIn. With LinkedIn you've got a profile already up there and you can immediately go in and look at someone else's and get far more information than you ever would have if you'd turned up at a meeting five or six years ago.

It gives you an opportunity to increase brand identity or send a message or offer at the flick of a switch instead of having to print out lots of letters. You can stay competitive by sending out messages each day and certainly have a strong influence on company image by addressing complaints or any negative comments really quickly.

How to manage your social marketing

With Facebook and B2B, you really want to become the industry resource or thought leader in your industry and share insights. Engage with the community and ask for feedback. Don't just keep posting information up there. Actually ask for comment.

Expand beyond your wall. Get comments on Facebook to drive, for example, to your LinkedIn site or to your website. What you're doing is you're creating a community that is engaging with you through different media. You might even advertise a seminar on Facebook, and they come through and meet you. Lighten up! Spark interest and have a bit of fun. It doesn't all have to be boring.

This is one of my loves: B2B blogging. Blogs are a wonderful way for businesses to drive thought leadership programs and really cut through and make a splash via influencers. We've got blogs being used by businesses for marketing, branding, public relations, tech support, education, competitive edge, research and recruitment. There's a real opportunity to be able to use blogs as a very strategic tool and they give a great opportunity to enhance the image of our organizations.

I used to send an email newsletter out once a month. These days I speak to 60,000 on ninemsn through a blog and it takes me an hour, whereas doing a newsletter used to take ages to research, write, design, approve and get out. If people aren't commenting, then the blog needs to be redirected, and you can only do that by trial and error. For example, I find on my ninemsn blog that if I mention anything political, I immediately get a big response. It's interesting.

Certain topics spark certain readers, but you do need to keep trialing until you find the right equation.

Twitter is pretty amazing too. In the B2B world, Twitter is a great tool to use to fix complaints or to address sales enquiries. If you hashtag your business keywords in your tweets, you can catch people who are looking for your products and services, as well as people who are complaining. Look at these stats: 200 million users, 65 million tweets a day. It's huge. You can network with your customers. You can promote their image and yours. You can get customer feedback and certainly address any complaints really quickly with Twitter.

YouTube is moving to be the new norm; if you're promoting it, you need to video it and get it up on YouTube. It's the most extraordinary platform for promoting and educating. Anybody can load a little 30-second video now and within days, if it's good, it can go viral and you can get millions looking at it. YouTube really should be front of mind for any companies now who are looking to educate, promote or communicate. There are some dreadful YouTube videos up and some good ones, and again, it's trial and error. One of the ways that the Old Spice campaign started–if you remember "the man that you'd like your man to smell like"–started with YouTube and was extraordinarily successful.

LinkedIn has over 100 million registered users. This is *the* B2B tool. If you're in business and you're not on LinkedIn, then I suggest you get to that really quickly. LinkedIn is your Facebook for business. Get the LinkedIn profile that you have up to 100 percent. Don't have it sitting there at 50 or 60 percent. Have it completely filled out with all your keywords of what you do. Then when people search for you or search for your services, you'll be coming up first.

LinkedIn has the most extraordinary search engine optimization capability, so if your LinkedIn profile is full and complete, whether you pay for SEO or not, when someone searches for your services, LinkedIn is the thing that comes up first. LinkedIn is a must-do. Everybody should be on there.

Be consistent. Don't tweet for a day and then never tweet again. Don't set one blog up and never again. Get a consistent pattern and whatever that frequency is, make sure it's within your competency. There's nothing worse than having someone speak out about something they know nothing about. Remember that social media is our new B2B. It's too good to ignore. Innovation, new opportunities? How lucky are we!

Cydney's Social Wealth Action steps:

1. Set up your professional Twitter account. Take the time to follow at least 100 people whose advice you value. Check our website, www. MillionairesAcademy.com/Resources, for service providers offering social media branded account profiles.

2. Set up a service to link your Twitter and Facebook posts so that you can automate some of your social media efforts. Check our website for the latest services. At the time of writing, we are using Hootsuite, which comes in both free and paid versions.

3. If you do not have a blog already, then hire someone to set one up for you now. Make sure it can be linked in with your automation and syndication system so you post to both your blog and your social media accounts automatically.

4. If you already have a blog and have not found the time or desire to post to it, allocate the task to someone on your team or a contractor who can be relied upon to get the job done.

5. If you do not already have one, create a LinkedIn account. If you do have one, now is the time to review your profile and invite everyone in your email list to connect with you. I recently did this and connected with thousands of powerful influencers in a matter of days.

CHAPTER 13

SOCIAL BRAND POWER: DOMINATE YOUR MARKET IN 90 DAYS

Ben Angel

Personal Branding and Influence Expert, Author and Speaker

Ben Angel, "The Angel of Influence," is an author and business and lifestyle columnist. As a visual communications and marketing specialist on personal branding, he grooms his clients in how to be more seductive to their target market. A busy professional speaker, Ben has delivered presentations for major organizations including Toyota, Australia Post, the Australian Institute of Company Directors and Origin Energy. Ben's media exposure includes Australian national TV networks and publications such as The Australian, The Herald Sun, Channel 9 and ABC Radio. He is the author of two books, Sleeping Your Way to the Top and Sleeping Your Way to the Top in Business.

It's easier to rule from the top!

We use media because it's one of the fastest ways to dominate your industry, build your profile, increase your credibility and sell more products and services. But there are major marketing mistakes that people make, such as:

- Guessing what works. You need to actually find out what's working within your industry. What are the marketing techniques? What is the science behind them?
- Sporadic marketing attempts, not having a clear, distinct plan to follow. You must use key fundamental marketing activities to make sure your pipeline is consistently filled with prospective clients.
- Zero marketing strategy. You need to have some kind of process or plan in place for what is going to occur, not only within the next 90 days but within the next 12 months and even into the next 5 years. You need to understand where you are taking this business.
- Failing to invest in education. Invest in further education around marketing. The education that you gain will last you a lifetime and also make you more profitable.
- **Time Management - I would say for 90 percent of the marketing techniques we apply; we have automated all of the processes, email campaigns, follow-up, even Facebook and social media processes. Automating these processes makes sure that marketing is consistently going up and we're not dropping the ball in any key area.**

Fitness indicators

Fitness indicators are a signal of one's individual traits and qualities that are recognized by others. They play a specific role in our lives: to attract mates, solicit assistance from parents, kin and community and to deter predators and intimidators. Everyone fakes fitness indicators in one form or another; such as wearing makeup, driving specific cars, or name dropping. We do it daily, not only to assert our status but also to make sure we have a place.

Human beings have two main objectives: to achieve some kind of status and to experience pleasure. So how can people achieve their status or pleasure by purchasing your products or services? Products and services are a direct reflection and expression of who we are as an individual. Whether or not you choose to wear brand name clothing is an example of an expression of your personal style.

The Domination Model

The Domination Model is one I personally utilize for my own business and for my own my clients as well. It's in three steps. We have profile, which is building a profile of a personal brand, as well as the overall business. Second, we have publicity, and publicity isn't just national media coverage; publicity could also be through Facebook, Twitter, YouTube, writing articles, emailing out to your database. The third step is profits; we have to make sure all of our activities are profitable. I'm going to delve into the topic I've being really focusing on for over seven years now: personal branding.

There are over 11 million bits of information coming into the brain at any given second. Our conscious mind can only record 3 to 4. When it comes to marketing, we have to make sure we're only deliver 3 to 4 bits of information, not more, or we'll lose the sale.

Perception is reality

The reason why someone will actually purchase from your business is because they can express themselves through your product or service. If you're like every other product or service in the industry, there's no real reason for them to purchase through you. Instead of buying on perceived value, they will shop around on price. When you have a distinct message and you are niched in your industry, people will perceive you as more valuable.

The formula we work on is message plus perception equals reality, because reality is really in the eyes of the beholder. So the message that you're taking to the marketplace will have individuals perceive you and treat you in a specific way.

There are over 11 million bits of information coming into the brain at any given second. The subconscious mind takes 40 to 60 bits of information and pushes it forward to our conscious mind. Our conscious mind can only record 3 to 4 bits of information for up to 20 seconds before we actually have to recommit it to memory. So when it comes to marketing, we have to make sure that we're only delivering 3 to 4 bits of information, not more, because that will lose your sale. We have to really simplify it. So what are the 3 to 4 bits of information that you're projecting through your styling, what you wear, and your body positioning?

Whether we're a speaker, an author, a business owner, a service provider or we're selling products, we not only need to look at the message that the overall business is taking to the marketplace, we need to look at the message that *we're* taking to the marketplace. Any good marketing consultant will look at a business and go, "Okay, what are the top three brand values of this business?"

When it comes to personal branding we need to ask ourselves, what are the top three brand values that we hold as a personal brand? Your personal brand is communicated through your message; it's communicated through your look, behavior, interaction, authenticity and also consistency. Are you switching and changing on an ongoing basis so that no one really has a clear understanding of what it is that you actually do? My definition of personal branding is self-expression, amplified, to influence and command attention.

Personal style

Your style indicates you have status and how you view yourself and your individuality. I can tell you immediately how you feel about yourself by the clothes that you've chosen to wear. Clothes distort our body. A lot of black will shrink us; it will also make us look frumpier in some instances depending on how it's worn. Clothes distort the body and the message. We can make ourselves look bigger. We can thin ourselves down as well. We can make ourselves look more vibrant.

For example, if you were suffering from depression, which is something that I have suffered from in the past, there is never a point where I would wear red because it's the brightest color you could possibly wear and would draw attention to me, which I didn't want in that point of time. So I always hid myself in black. If we want to stand out and we're feeling really great about ourselves we will tend to wear brighter colors than darker colors.

When the moment is brief, the impact needs to be profound, especially around our personal brand. When it comes to social media, it's become even more important that you get your personal style right. If we look at this from a psychological perspective, our subconscious mind literally seeks to find a fit between the way that someone looks and the role that they play in our lives.

When the moment is brief, the impact needs to be profound.

Your personal style will help you achieve instant credibility, assist in increasing your conversion rates and generate immediate results. I'm not expecting everyone to be suited up constantly; a lot of people assume that you have to be in a suit. You need to be at least the best dressed or the second best dressed person in attendance when you're at a business meeting or with a client.

Social proof

Social proof and credibility may come from testimonials from your clients. It may come from visual imagery such as pictures of yourself speaking in front of an audience, it might come from avenues other than media. Once you have media, it is all about making sure that you extend that reach. Once you expand and leverage it, you will see that your status increases significantly and you start to collect a different kind of social proof.

If you're in a magazine, for example, or you have written an article that goes out to a magazine of 30,000-plus people, the assumption is that the magazine has deemed you credible enough to put you in front of 30,000 people. That social proof will generate you a lot of money over the years. You use the media to increase your influence and conversion rates overall, which also helps you attract top paying clients and dominate your market within a very short period of time.

Media exposure will increase your conversion rates. A great technique I use for speaking engagements is I will give them a magazine or a newspaper that's had a featured article on me or a relevant story about me and say, "Here's a featured article I thought you might be interested in."

Accelerated wealth secret:
The 90-Day Domination Challenge

The 90-Day Domination Challenge is really broken up into three core parts. The first is building a foundation. In month one the foundation is all about ensuring you have your marketing materials in order, you have a strong personal branding message. If you want media exposure, you've been writing your press releases and know which media you're about to target, you have your marketing strategy in place; the website is up-to-date and everything is in place.

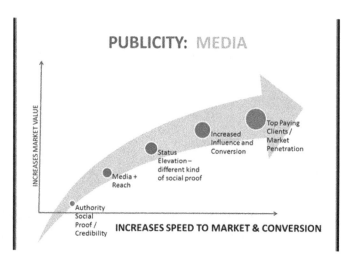

> You must have key fundamental marketing activities
> occurring 24/7 to make sure that your pipeline is
> consistently filled with prospective clients.

Month two we are full force. You take it to market. You make sure that you get as much exposure as you possibly can get in a finite amount of time. We do this because a lot of businesses do a sporadic marketing attempt, it's here, it's nine months later, three months after that… no consistent ongoing exposure, not having a clear plan to follow.

A lot of businesses do some marketing, get a lot of clients, get really busy and then won't have time to do any marketing. So the marketing ball gets completely dropped. They got funds and all of the sudden they realize they have run out of clients. They start marketing again. They are going through this whole up-and-down rollercoaster-type ride throughout their business journey.

Whether you get busy or not, you must have key fundamental marketing activities occurring 24/7 to make sure that your pipeline is consistently filled with prospective clients. When you do, you're not only able to build a profile of the business up, you will be build your own profile, your personal brand, attract publicity and increase your profits.

Working in music stores I used to watch artists release a new album or single. They would literally have a seven-day period to make that single go to number one. In Australia, at that point in time, you only needed to sell about 800 singles in one week to get a number one song, a lot less than people think it is. The way a musician markets a new album, they will do as much radio media promotion and performances as they possibly can within a short amount of time. For some artists it might be a three-month process, so we see promotions before the album comes out and of course there is a full-on promotion as soon as it hits the shelves as well.

Month three is about making sure that whatever critical mass we've built up from month two we leverage as much as possible. So if you've had media exposure in month two, then in month three you're letting your database know about that media exposure on Facebook, Twitter and YouTube and everywhere else. Then leave that database alone, be quiet for a month or two, then build up to something big once again. This is an important process to understand: that we always have to be going through this cycle and building up the excitement.

If no one is purchasing from you right now, it's most likely that they don't enough value in the product or service that you're offering. The way to shift that is by changing the message using social proof, media, speaking and networking in your industry.

Cydney's Social Wealth Action steps:

1. Search for yourself and your company using all of the major search engines. Have a really good look at what comes up. Is this what you want your ideal or dream clients to see when they check you out?

2. Is it clear what problem your business solves and how to get that solution? Are there compelling calls to action for prospects to buy into your business?

3. Make a list of 10 things you can do to improve the message that communicates what your company offers and why you're the best choice.

4. Review your own brand and style. Is it current, attractive and engaging? Does it relay the most appropriate message? Does your website work properly with the search engines?

5. Plan your own "90-Day Challenge" to boost sales and exposure.

CHAPTER 14

NEW BRAND RULES FOR MARKET LEADERS

Kim Castle

CEO, Intention Products;
BrandU® Co-Creator

Kim Castle is CEO of Intention Products and co-creator of BrandU®. For nearly a decade, hera revolutionary three-stage business development system, often dubbed the "E-myth® for a new generation of business" has been guiding thousands of entrepreneurs and small business owners to grow beyond the confusion of possibility to the power of extreme clarity, from "idea" to their million dollar brand. She and her collaborator and partner, W. Vito Montone, have worked alongside Fortune 500 companies such as General Motors, Wolfgang Puck, IBM, M&M's, Disney and Paramount, and have had their hands in products grossing $100 million. Through their Interprise™ Business Incubator they guide entrepreneurs around the world to turn their ideas into million dollar brands, creating businesses they love and can rely on for life.

The New Frontier

The 21st century is an exciting time to be in business. Never before has the playing field been so level; via the Internet, both start-ups and global corporations can now cost-effectively reach a global audience–if they know the rules for this new economy.

With these opportunities, however, come new challenges, the largest being: How does any business stand out when there are millions of websites competing for attention over dozens of new distribution channels? Long-established marketing strategies are failing and many businesses don't understand why.

To succeed in this new economy, every company, no matter how small, must create a viable brand—one that people connect to, one that will bring them back again and again to buy what the company is selling. This is true today more than at any other time in history.

Why? Because a new economy has evolved, driven in equal measure by the rise of social media, by an intense and prolonged global economic downturn and by the seismic shift in expectations among consumers. Massive layoffs have created thousands of new entrepreneurs competing to attract consumers who no longer buy anything that looks interesting, but only what they perceive to be valuable. For these newcomers, and for established businesses struggling to adjust, the new economy demands a new way of approaching "brand," a sadly misunderstood concept.

No company is too small to develop their brand;
in fact success demands it from day one.

Branding is the act of taking your message out to the consumer...on a Frisbee, a pen, or on the side of a bus. It's the act of getting your brand seen. *Developing a brand* means building something people will connect to for a lifetime. It is intrinsic to the core of your business and will directly determine your ability to reliably grow your business in the coming years by being so clear that you can cut straight through the mass of marketing noise.

A brand is the precise and pinpointed communication of your company, your product or service, the value that it stands for and the ongoing feeling that customers consistently get from it. It's about everything that you do – every choice you make, every partner you bring on. No company is too small to develop their brand; in fact, success demands it from day one.

You can begin today by following these five brand rules for the new economy:

Brand rule #1: Lead

Many marketers have said, "Find out what the market needs and then sell it." That approach may have worked in the dawn of Internet marketing, but it's not sustainable. News, information and trends simply move too fast to stay ahead of such flux. Apple CEO Steve Jobs summed it up perfectly: "You can't just ask customers what they want and then try to give that to them. By the time you get it built, they'll want something new."

In order to command customer attention and loyalty, the new economy demands that you, the entrepreneur, get out in front with products and services that are innovative and become a vital part of consumers' lives. That comes from developing the "right" business. The right business for you is one that connects to your core, that you love being a part of and that solves a problem you are uniquely suited to solve. We all are uniquely suited to solve at least one problem and are on the path to solving it.

Entrepreneurs who uncover their path turn into passionate communicators and are unstoppable in attracting the people who are best suited for their products and services. That inner passion is what sets your brand apart from everyone else and what frees you from trying to imitate your competitors. This has been proved by many successful companies: Whole Foods, The Container Store, Apple and so many more.

Brand rule #2: One-to-many

In order to truly thrive in the new economy, you must understand how we got here.

Commerce began as a one-to-one relationship between buyer and seller–trading a goat for a haircut, a rug for a chicken. The Industrial Revolution enabled mass production of products, removing any connection to the seller. The emphasis was on the product and the business owner's primary focus was on making affordable products.

Benefiting from systems innovation and mass distribution honed over previous decades, the Internet Age shifted the emphasis off of products and onto people. The prominent focus was on market reach–in fact, in many respects, the product didn't matter.

In the new economy we've come full circle, but with a twist. We are returning to the direct association with the seller, re-establishing the ancient one-on-one relationship, although it's not just with one person, it's with many consumers thanks to social media. And not just any consumers, either, but those people who best align with what the business is selling. Trying to be all things to all people is a guaranteed strategy for failure.

Trying to be all things to all people is a guaranteed strategy for failure.

Brand rule #3:
Be prepared to deliver the whole meal

For decades, marketers have been told to "sell the sizzle, not the steak." This comes from the glittery golden age of advertising with its flashy cars, celebrity endorsements, glamour and glitz galore. Underneath, the product often disappointed when the excitement wore off, creating a whole generation of consumers who have grown wary of "flash." In short, companies failed to create value in the product, only the "promise" of it via the advertising.

Disillusioned consumers wary of being disappointed by "the sizzle" are now demanding the steak, three side dishes and dessert, and want to know everything about the meal including where it came from and why it exists, plus a guarantee. It can't just smell like coffee and come in a pretty cup; if you want to charge five bucks for a cup, it had better be great coffee, in a useful cup, delivered with a smile, piping hot, in an environment that creates a memorable experience. Starbucks understands this.

Brand rule #4: It has to be real

Modern consumers can smell when something's not real. The sizzling smokescreen doesn't work anymore–actually, it never did long-term. In the new economy, people are more discerning regarding how to spend their money. That means, you–and your product–need to establish a connection with your customers that wins their loyalty and keeps them coming back. They need to trust in the promise of a good brand, that it offers them real connection and value for their time and money.

Brand rule #5: There needs to be more

We all want to feel that we have given our money and our loyalty to something worthwhile. The fly-by-night marketer earns our contempt because he has stolen our trust along with our cash. Your brand must stand for something, whether it answers a need in our society, helps the environment, or is simply good clean fun. Every single thing you do builds a brand impression in the minds of your customers, from the quality of the products to the outlets where you choose to sell them.

A brand done well is rooted deep inside the founder. It engages people and keeps them coming back with a personal attachment to your brand, your products or services. Everyone who comes in contact with your brand should get from it a clear understanding of what you stand for: your culture, your values, your brand soul...the things you are passionate about solving.

> Everyone who comes into contact with your brand should get from it a clear understanding of what you stand for: your culture, your values, your brand soul.

In the new economy, a small business can literally change the world by providing independence for its owner and jobs for others, money for charitable causes and new products to shape the world around us. All of that is tied directly to the brand and its DNA, because it is the brand that people ultimately trust... and in the new economy, trust spells the difference between a vital, thriving business and one that is perpetually skating on the edge and never understanding why.

By following these rules, you can be sure that you'll have what it takes to not only survive in the coming age of business, but to thrive.

As an entrepreneur, you have the power to change the world because you have the power to dream, to believe, to not take "no" for an answer and to take action on an idea and run with it all the way to the bank. As a business owner, a business leader, you can change everything in your life, your family's life and the world around you by becoming a truly stable entity through your business, by fulfilling your own independence.

In this new economy, the world needs you. It needs your business to succeed, and the great news is that you don't have to do it alone. But you do need to decide one thing: that you are ready to lead.

Cydney's Social Wealth Action Steps:

1. As a leader in your business, (if you don't think you are, change your thinking), take a good, long look at your business. Is it the right business? Does it fit you? Do you genuinely solve a problem for others in a valuable way?

2. What can you do to improve the solutions you offer, do you really understand all your customer's problems related to your solutions?

3. Look at your products and services. Are you selling the sizzle or the steak? How are your client retentions, and repeat sales rates? Is your business focused on delighting the customers you have or finding new ones? Where should it be?

4. What is the relationship of your brand with your market?

5. Based on the answers to these questions, draft 10 areas for improvement that you can implement over the next 3-12 months. Remember to include timelines, deadlines and accountabilities.

SECTION THREE

CONNECT

Social Media, it turns out, isn't about aggregating audiences so you can yell at them about the junk you want to sell. Social Media, in fact, is a basic human need, revealed digitally online. We want to be connected, to make a difference, to matter, to be missed. We want to belong, and yes, we want to be led.

— **Seth Godin,** SethGodin.typepad.com

CHAPTER 15

FINDING YOUR AUTHENTIC CONNECTION

Tania Usher

Founder and CEO, Tania Usher
International

Tania Usher is often called the "Queen of Connection" and is internationally renowned for her "Get NAKED" philosophies for uncovering your authentic success mindset. Tania left her jetsetting corporate career in marketing communications, tragically lost her firstborn son, then gave birth to two healthy daughters. She became the sole provider for her family, witnessed escalating credit card debt and was served home repossession papers. After several challenges becoming a home based entrepreneur, she built a strong team and systems and her life is very different now; she runs her media and mentoring business from a beautiful beachfront home and office.

Today thousands of people follow Tania online and her events have touched the lives of over 100,000 people from a variety of industries and nations. Living on purpose, Tania's vision is to inspire heart-centered women around the world to create a dynamic life doing what they love while having lots of fun. "Boring is out" is Tania's motto. Featured regularly in the media including recent appearances on the Today Show, Tania believes that nurturing relationships and making soulful connections is the key to success.

Get controversial and get attention!

In 2009 I launched my e-zine with the title: "Get NAKED with Tania" that followed on with the business and lifestyle advice from workshops I had done. I used the title to stand out in a noisy world. It was an experiment, a small newsletter. I didn't have a list, so I invited my contacts on Outlook to connect. I was amazed because hundreds of people from around the world signed up within hours. The feedback was that I got their attention with the "Get NAKED with Tania" title.

The e-zine goes out once a week and within twelve months, I'd created a 10,000-strong community, not just with my e-zine, but it was a stepping stone. When you create a compelling reason for people to connect with you, initially they may be intrigued and curious. However, with regular connection, a stronger relationship is forged.

If I have an event coming up–a product launch, a new book or something quite specific–as well as including details in my e-zine and social networking sites, I send an individual broadcast email. My experience as well as extensive research by others indicates that these solo broadcasts receive higher open rates.

The biggest mistake that entrepreneurs
make is that they promote way too much.

Online vs. offline communication

One of the most powerful and cost-effective communication tools is leveraging free publicity. It's been a great strategy to build my community. Third-party endorsements are always very powerful, particularly from the media. It's an effective strategy both online and offline; bloggers, journalists and e-zine publishers are always looking for content. When you are profiled in somebody else's publication, it's a great way to build your credibility, although the biggest mistake that entrepreneurs make is that they promote way too much. They fail to share engaging stories. The more stories you share, the more media coverage you enjoy. I've been profiled in a host of different magazines on numerous topics from parenting and losing a child, to what kind of heels to wear in the summer, fashion wars at the school gates, healthy eating and business. My "story box" boasts a variety of topics.

Being profiled in one medium can lead to exposure in another. The feature article on fashion wars is a great example. Producers of the *Today Show* read the feature and invited us to do a story for them, which we did. During the filming I got speaking with the journalist, telling her about some of my clients and about one of my events Connecting Mumpreneurs. She was keen to know more and within a few weeks I was profiling two clients on the *Today Show*.

The story angle is really what piques the interest of journalists, that's how we've managed to get so much publicity. I also write a monthly column in Australia's most widely distributed magazine focusing on kids. It has 150,000 subscribers online and offline. That's amazing leverage because people read about you in the magazine. Writing a regular feature or column is a great way to boost credibility and exposure. If you're a keen writer, then keep your eye out for new magazine launches. Most publications are hungry for stories, so show them what you've got. I've written for a number of different magazines and I essentially I invite myself to be a contributing writer. The key is to speak up.

Accelerated wealth secret:
Live events and social marketing

Events are a fantastic way to build your community. A great way to get started with your first event is to leverage off of something else that's happening. International Women's Day was a great opportunity for us. We created what started out as a one-day forum for women to celebrate International Women's Day and ended up creating a festival that hosted 14 events over 9 days. With events, I recommend you don't over plan and perfect. Throw your heart into the first one then tweak along the way. The important thing is to get started and do the first one. As you become more experienced and learn more about your audience, you begin to implement systems. Events are very time consuming, so you have to have systems and the right support; otherwise, you'll burn out.

As a connector and event organizer, social marketing is an intrinsic part of my business. Having seen the success of online marketing and social networking, as a business owner it would be foolish to not have an online presence. You're just going to be left behind without it. For me, it's a combination of social media and events; there's nothing greater than that face-to-face communication. What

I see on social media is all these people wanting to be your friend and you have no idea who they are. There's no connection; that's just name collecting.

It makes sound business sense to look for inexpensive or free marketing strategies and social marketing is one of those. It's a fantastic way to get your message out there. I share different things, various business and personal transformations. My business recently underwent a rebranding which is very exciting. From this we launched our online magazine, *Dare*, and sharing the journey with my audience has been encouraging and fun.

There is enough happening in your world and the world around you that there is no need to worry about lack of content. Keep connected with your community by sharing some of your day-to-day activities. Of course, privacy is an issue so I don't suggest revealing the deeply personal unless it's part of the story you share and you've made a strategic decision to do so. Your community wants to be taken inside your world, so share the stuff that humanizes you, which is important in this wired world of ours. Social media and my e-zine have enabled me to connect more deeply with my community. Providing the opportunity to communicate, comment and engage allows your community to get involved and share their expertise. This giving and receiving creates the space for your audience to also give back to you.

> Your community wants to be taken inside your world, so share the stuff that humanizes you, which is important in this wired world of ours.

Social media allows you to share some of those personal elements that are important to all of us. Without them, the risk is that you're not connecting at all and instead what you have is a technical relationship.

Protecting your intellectual property

While it is very important to protect the security of your brand, many people spend way too much time worrying about their competition. This is wasted energy because the fact is there is no competition. No one can create, deliver and operate a business the same way you do. Somebody may copy my information, duplicate my events and even plagiarize my material and no matter how much of that they do, they will never be able to deliver products and services the way I do. They're not me.

Do take steps to keep your intellectual property safe. Use copyright symbols and trademarking wherever you need to and keep an eye on your competition. However, conserve your energy for enhancing the customer experience; that's what's going to protect your brand. They're going to know that you're the real deal and you're authentic, as opposed to somebody else who comes to try to do a knockoff. The copycat strategy will never last as it doesn't come from a heart-driven philosophy and so lacks the DNA necessary for success.

The only thing stopping people from reaching
the success they crave is their own self-doubt.

Tips for success

It's important to make space for creativity to flow. One powerful way of doing this is to pause every few months, stop and reassess. During the pause, start extracting overgrown weeds or thoughts or ideas in your head. Be prepared to make mid-course adjustments. Strategy A may have been a great social networking strategy last month, but it may be redundant several months down the road.

Adopting a success mindset is essential for success. The only thing stopping people from reaching the success they crave is their own self-doubt. For me, entrepreneurship is one of the most powerful self-development journeys on which anybody can embark. Couple the success mindset with powerful masterminding, insightful mentoring and action taking, and success follows. I've never known a chapter of my life that has been as self-reflective as entrepreneurship. Nonetheless, success isn't a solo project and we need to work together.

Individuals have immense power individually, yet together we're unstoppable. When you work together with others you'll achieve far more than alone. The success of your business and your life is found by surrounding yourself with the right support. With that support you become energized, inspired and motivated, knowing you're not going it alone. Connecting with likeminded people encourages you to step more fully into your power.

Here's your challenge...

Step off that treadmill and stop. This may be confronting because your mind cries, "If I stop, then I'm not generating income." And if that's a fear then it is a definite indicator that you *must* stop. For your personal wellbeing and the wellbeing of your family, you need to be able to step out of the business, take a break and the business will continue to generate income. If that's not your story, then it's time to reevaluate the business model you're working with as it's not working for you. Generating passive income is essential for ongoing success. So take the time now to stop, reflect and create, even if it has an impact on your cash flow. When you regroup, energized, clearer and more connected with yourself, you'll have powerful tools for connecting with your community. The short-term tightening of wallets will serve you well in the long term.

Cydney's Social Wealth Action Steps:

1. Would a controversial campaign inject some life into your marketing? Consider engaging professional help if you're considering controversy, but it can be very powerful for getting attention.

2. Assign an appropriate team member to review the topical and important news stories in your community or industry. Are there opportunities to engage with the community through live event or expo sponsorship or participation, or renting a booth at a street festival?

3. Run a competition and engage your professional network to offer prizes or sponsorship. Competitions work really well for engaging social networking communities.

4. Create a mastermind group within your network to meet regularly and share "best of breed" ideas to improve your business performance and creativity.

5. Volunteer to write articles for a relevant magazine or trade journal, or guest blog on relevant, high readership blogs. Engage a writer to create the articles if you don't have the time, talent or desire. We have a staff of writers and a press release team, so check out www. MillionairesAcademy.com/Resources if you need help in this area.

CHAPTER 16

21ST CENTURY COMMUNICATION

Lorrie Morgan Ferrero

Founder and CEO, Red Hot Copy

Lorrie Morgan-Ferrero founded Red Hot Copy in 1999 so she could work anywhere, raise her family and still make a good living. Her background in journalism and acting prepared her for the creative (and competitive) nature of copywriting. After studying closely with master copywriters, Lorrie has become a world-renowned and award-winning copywriter with her own unique style. She has an uncanny ability to make her copy bond and build relationships with the prospect, driving them to become loyal customers buying from her (or her clients) over and over again. From her past reporter days, she is adamant about deeply researching the current industries, trends and competition. Her "Tarket" methodology has become part of the 21st century marketing lingo. After working closely with high profile speakers and entrepreneurs, Lorrie now focuses her passion on educating business owners in reaching the female market. She authored The She Factor based on her own She Factor Marketing System.

Softer selling for "She Success"

Things have changed in the marketing world, my friends. What worked in the 20th century has shifted and I'm going to be talking a lot about masculine versus feminine copy. I'm not saying that to be a gender-basher on any level.

What I'm talking about is depolarizing copy, taking it from that 20th century masculine, traditional "hypey" copy into relationship-building, friendlier, softer yet still selling, feminine version. Think of it as traditional versus modern.

I'll share with you eight differences between masculine versus feminine copy. There are more differences than I have pinpointed, but this has become my mission. I am really pioneering this area as far as shifting from the more masculine to the feminine.

- American women spend $5 to 7 trillion annually.
- Women head 40 percent of all households.
- Women represent 50 percent of Internet users but buy more online than men.
- Even though many households are dual paycheck, women still spend 80 percent of both incomes.
- Seventy percent of all new businesses are opened by women.
- Single women drive 20 percent of all home sales today.

Copywriting and marketing has shifted from being mass-produced and reaching out to lots of people. Where words are, you're going to find copy. Today it represents what your message is to your marketplace, to your community. I like to call it your community because today things are much more relationship-bound.

Silent no more

Let's go back in time to 1925 to 1942. Women and men had very defined roles in the household and in the economy. Women were called the silent generation, and they were. They were the homemakers. But with the advent of the Internet and the expansion of women in the economic fields, we had more choices and fairly recently, we have been getting more education. Fifty-seven percent more of the college degrees go to women. Seventy percent of all new businesses are opened by women. My personal feeling is because the Internet has opened up so many doors for people, it's much easier to open up your own business and to work virtually.

I became a copywriter when my corporate job ended. My boss retired and I had just remarried and I had two children. I really wanted to be home with those children. They suffered because I wasn't around, and I suffered. There was a lot of stress. I got us into $46,000 in debt in a very short period of time because I didn't know how to run a business. It was a crash course. It was like a college education, frankly, in business, in Internet.

I got a great client who wanted a copywriter. I didn't even know what a copywriter was, but I loved the style. I looked around to find training and there was nothing. This was back in the early 2000s; now, there's more opportunity. I was one of the very first women on the scene in the Internet world, especially in information marketing, in a group of men. It was a very male-dominated market. I found out who the best of the best were, the most successful, the million-dollar copywriting gurus and masters. I hired them to be my mentors. We've become friends and we collaborate together and discuss things.

I really got down how to be a good copywriter, but then the rules started changing. Copy is recycled. Copy that works well is perfectly acceptable to be used again in a different industry, in a different format. Copywriters model what has worked in the past.

♀ vs. ♂

Here are eight differences that I've isolated. There are many more in products that I have on my site, or if you see me speaking in person.

The first one: men and women respond to marketing language differently, so here's the first difference. In masculine copy, it's very emotionally aggressive. It's about "Kill your competition," "Stand at the top of the mountain and shout 'Victory,'" "Stand on the backs of the small people."

In feminine copy, they need a little more emotionally-bonding language. It doesn't mean you throw out good salesmanship, what it means is you need to build their trust. That may take more than one sales letter or one email. In fact, I'm pretty sure it will. The emotionally-bonding language that you use in feminine copy usually takes a bit longer to get to where you build that trust.

Masculine copy often mimics the offline direct response copy, where uglier is better. That worked for a long time. What I'm talking about with offline direct response is print. If you're going through your mailbox standing over the trash, throwing things away and you see the shiny brochure of window shutters– toss, toss–then maybe you see something that's ugly; it looks like somebody just wrote it on an old-fashioned typewriter and sent it to you on a yellow postcard. That might stand out a little bit more.

In masculine copy, values of the company are nice, but not necessarily a factor in making a buying decision. It's really more about, "I need this duct tape and here it is. It doesn't really matter to me that they kill baby seals in the process. I just don't think about it, I just buy the duct tape."

In feminine copy, it's very important. Anybody she does business with, she wants to know that you're a good person, that you're not one of those bad companies that are spilling oil in the ocean or doing things that are politically incorrect. It makes a difference. So the point for you is if you have a charity or you do good stuff, you need to include that somewhere in your copy, include that in your brand and what it's all about.

In masculine copy, stories are good. Guys like stories, but they're not critical. Sometimes they just get in the way and the guys get impatient. They want to cut to the chase and know what's going on. They don't want to hear about how you got into business.

Feminine copy is a little different. Stories are actually required to catch her attention and to bond. It's all about bonding. When I started telling you the story of how I got into copywriting, did you pay closer attention or not? I know when I'm watching people, or listening to people, and they start telling me their story or a story that's related to their point, I listen more attentively. It's human nature to do that, especially with women.

In masculine copy, men are generally looking for one solution. When my husband goes to Home Depot or to a "man's store," he's usually got an idea of one thing he's going to get. It's not like batching everything that he's going to need on one trip. If he needs a wrench, he's going for a wrench. He's not going to go for a wrench and also a plant and some air freshener. He's going into the store for one solution.

In masculine copy, facts and figures are very important in making a buying decision. They want to know the percentage of your success, the dollar amount of your growth and whatever the statistics are for this and that. Those can be impressive, but for women and feminine copy, personalities and stories are much more alive to them than facts and figures. They're actually more important when it comes to selling to women, to marketing to women.

Getting to know your "your tarket"

The next thing I want to share is one of my favorite things. It's my secret for building relationships with copy. What I'm going to share with you is something that I actually developed by accident, but it has been the difference when it comes to making my copy sound connecting, making the person on the other side of that copy feel like I'm talking directly to them. You can do this too. I'm going to explain to you exactly how.

[My secret] has been the difference in making the person on the other side of the copy feel like I'm talking directly to them.

What I'm talking about is a term that I've coined called a "tarket." What the heck is a tarket? You've heard of target market. A target market to me sounds like a mob. It's the group of people you want to do business with and when you write to a mob, it's very depersonalized.

That doesn't work in copy. In copy, you need to build a relationship and to make the person on the other end feel important and that you're talking to her directly. A "tarket" is a single person. I encourage you to do something like this for yourself, for your own target market, for your own "tarket," and I'll give you some hints on how to do that.

My recommendation is to write a little paragraph about your own tarket. The way you're going to find out this information is to look through your past database, your past customers, your ideal customers, the people you want to reach and just make a little snapshot of who that person is, to literally write up a little back story; a little persona, an avatar. They are all different terms that are used to describe a tarket.

Makeover example

Here are some makeovers that I want to share with you that can move your copy into the 21st century. I'm hoping that the before and afters I share will help you look at your own copy and mold it and soften it, and understand why you should act on the suggestions I'm about to give you.

The copy that you're going to read is copy that I personally wrote. I teach a virtual copywriting workshop and over the years it's evolved. The copy that I originally wrote was pretty masculine. It was the way I learned to write. Then I switched it up; let me show you what that looks like.

Original version: "What this bootcamp is not."

This is for the She Factor Copywriting Bootcamp. "What this bootcamp is not" is a reverse selling technique. I'll pull back the curtain and tell a little bit of my theories here.

The feminine makeover is "Before you make your decision, you should understand what this bootcamp is not." So you see there's a subtle difference, it's a little softer.

Quotes

People love quotes. You can actually hire an assistant to help you post these on a regular basis, to Facebook, to LinkedIn, to Twitter, to any of the gazillion other social media platforms, but I don't think you should get scattered using a lot of different social media platforms. That's why I personally focus in on Facebook and Twitter. LinkedIn is much more corporate and professional, but I'm noticing it's gaining ground pretty quickly. It has a lot of growth potential and a lot of reach.

When you don't know how to write copy,
you sacrifice speed to market.

Accelerated wealth secret:
Learn to write sales copy

Almost every successful guru I know knows how to write sales copy. It doesn't mean that they always do. Most of the time they do. They have to know how to evaluate it so they know if what they're looking at is any good. Imagine you hire a copywriter and they return copy to you, and you put in up on your website and nothing's happening. Maybe things are going gangbusters, but you don't know why, so how are you going to replicate that?

When you don't know how to write copy, you sacrifice speed to market. Let's say you have a fantastic idea in the middle of the night. You jump up in the morning to your computer, and now you have to find your copywriter, you have to get the wheels in motion. However if you have this idea and you know how to write copy, or you understand it, you can have a product, or the beginnings of a product, to market within a day, instead of having to stop and start, and lose your momentum.

This is fast, just giving you the gold. This is really the best of the best of what I know. I'm giving you five copywriting workouts to get good at creating copy fast. To get good at anything, you've got to actually do it. Just reading about it's not going to do, you have to do it physically, hands on, and so these little workouts stretch your brain very effortlessly, so you're able to get better at copy very quickly. If you're not in the right mindset when you're writing copy, it's really difficult. I've learned from mentoring with gurus, and actually having my own coaching programs, some tricks to tap into the winning mindset that you can use over and over again. They're things that I use to get myself on track, things that you can very easily use as well.

When it comes time to write your copy, you go to it and you look at it for inspiration. It's very important to see what triggers you and what is working out there in the marketplace. It doesn't have to just be in your industry, you can swipe files from boating magazines or from horse magazines or financial magazines or websites or mail.

The important thing is how they're getting their message across. Copywriting is a very psychological process. It's putting your message in a psychological format, in a certain order, that gets a certain reaction. It's not as mysterious as it sounds. I cover that very thoroughly in my "Quick Start Guide to Writing Red Hot Copy." I hope that you will use these tips, any of them, and that they give you wild success, and you'll continue studying your marketing and copywriting, and be a lifelong learner.

Get organic results with copy in social media

- How you write your search engine description is important. Prospects decide if they will even visit your site based on how your copy is written.
- Post business questions to your community. It builds trust, shows you're interested in feedback and positions you as the expert while creating dialogue.
- Give, give, give. Remember, you aren't selling in social media. You are building a relationship. In this case, it's not "the more you tell, the more you sell" but "the more you *share* the more you sell."
- Schedule your social media time. You can schedule tweets using different platforms like Hootsuite or hire an assistant to post business tidbits, quotes, etc. in Facebook.

Cydney's Social Wealth Action steps:

1. It's time to look at the communication style and language on your websites, blogs, brochures and social and offline media posts. Is the style appropriate to attract your ideal clients?

2. Does a masculine style suit your message, or is it time to start using a more conversational feminine touch in your communications? If you aren't sure, you can run surveys using both styles and see which ones get the better responses.

3. How many communication mediums are you using in your communications? Are your clients hearing from you through high-value video, audio, email, postal messages, welcome text messages and personal phone calls? If not, how can you improve their customer experience and incorporate more interactive experiences for them?

4. How well did you define your avatar in the first chapter of this book? It's now time to come back to that and review whom you have been attracting and actually working with versus whom you may have thought you were working with. Identify the clients you've been attracting and further define your "tarket."

5. Make sure you brief the team member responsible for creating your client and marketing communications; work with them to test and measure the results of various communications to identify which ones are producing results for you. Analyze those results so you can duplicate and improve upon on those results.

CHAPTER 17

HOW TO ROMANCE YOUR TRIBE

Janet Beckers

Founder and CEO,
Wonderful Web Women

On the day that Janet Beckers launched her Internet community, Wonderful Web Women, she had no list, no money and no track record. Within eight weeks she had built a community of thousands of people worldwide, matched her previous twelve months of income and won an award for best membership site. Since then, Janet has helped thousands of people create success online. She is a sought-after international speaker, best-selling author and mentor.

One of Janet's claims to fame is that she has achieved it all without spending a dime on advertising. Instead, she uses the power of relationships and communication to build an Internet business and teaches her many students how to quickly and easily create a business that makes you stand out in the crowd of millions of websites. She shows how to attract loyal and passionate customers that will grow your business for you. She teaches about online membership programs, group coaching, private mentoring and workshops in Australia and overseas. She is a multi-award winning entrepreneur, having most recently won Australian Marketer of the Year.

The art of online marketing

My background is in nursing. It taught me about how to communicate with people from all walks of life. I was working with small rural communities in Australia, bringing them together so they could look at health issues and what they could do about them.

I decided that when I had my babies, I didn't want to be working full time. I wanted to be able to work from home. That's when I started my first Internet business, which was an art gallery online. I was studying art to keep me sane when my children were babies and I thought, "There aren't many places to be able to exhibit your artwork. I'll start an Internet art gallery. I've heard you can make a lot of money on the Internet."

I had never run a business. I did not know what a business plan was. I didn't even know much about the Internet. I think I made every single mistake that you could possibly make running that. I can look back at those times and understand when people tell me their frustrations or problems. I can relate to every single one of them because I did it, too.

I had the webmasters from hell. I'd dealt with trying to understand how it all fits together, how you actually do marketing and how you create products. I learned from trial and error rather than doing the sensible thing of paying for a mentor to teach me how to do it.

The start of something wonderful

After a while, I went to my first Internet marketing conference. There were a couple of things that really struck me. One of those was there was so many different ways you could be successful on the Internet. One that appealed to me was creating an information product. You can create something once and sell it over and over again. I had been a consumer of information products, but never seen that I could be building a business around this. That was the first light bulb moment for me.

I sold the art gallery and then I spent the next year turning into a conference junkie, learning how to build a successful business on the Internet. I noticed going to all these conferences there were very few women on stage. There might be one or if there was a woman, she was in partnership with her husband.

The women in the audience were saying, "Where are the women? I need role models that I can relate to." That's where the idea of Wonderful Web Women was born. I was working with different people to set up their website business. I was learning a lot, but wasn't known as an expert in this area.

The Oprah effect

There are a couple of ways that you can build your business:

- Be the expert and create your training programs, services and products around your expertise.
- Be the reporter, like Oprah. She positioned herself as a go-to person.

So that's what I did with Wonderful Web Women; find the women who've created success online, interview them on live teleseminars, share their stories and create a community around that.

I chose the very best people and approached them. Within eight weeks, a really interesting thing happened. When you start your business this way and people hear you interviewing an expert, they think, Well, she must be an expert as well.

When people hear you interviewing an expert,
they think, Well, she must be an expert as well.

Within weeks people were emailing me saying, "Janet, can you please mentor me? I like what you've been doing. I can feel a real connection with you."

Understanding connection and community is how I successfully built my online business. It's through a process I call "romance your tribe." Why "tribe?" When it comes to the way that people interact, we tend to look for people who have similar interests and values. One way of thinking about that is as a tribe. There are five stages:

Flirting

You want to be showing yourself to be the best. You're being yourself, just a shiny you.

A mistake people sometimes make is they will be sharing things on social media that really are not doing anything to enhance their brand. Thinking about who is it that I'm trying to attract, who do I want to flirt with? Where am I going to find them? When you're deciding whether to be using Facebook versus Twitter versus LinkedIn, go to where your target market hangs out. If you're business to business or working with corporates, you want LinkedIn. If you're business to business and dealing with people who want to be developing a lot more trust with you, Facebook is a perfect medium.

In social media, look for the people in your niche who already have a high reputation with your target market. Start getting to know those people. The right way to do it is by going to their pages and asking intelligent questions, which gives them the opportunity to show how clever they are.

Come back to my place

No matter what industry you're in, I recommend that you have a blog. You might write about handy tips or articles, but give people the opportunity to know a bit more about you. Naturally move people through the process where they want to end up buying from you. It should be designed in a way that helps them work out that you can solve their problems.

We haven't been trying to make a sale yet. Let people know that you do have things for sale, but not putting the pressure on. You've just been inviting them back to your place.

With social media you can also interact. You can make your blog articles automatically load over to Facebook and Twitter, put links onto your blog to say, "If you like this article, click here," and put it out to Twitter and Facebook, so the traffic flows both ways.

Courting

It's still a one-way street. You're still doing the hard work. They're not quite sure if they're into you yet, but they have given you permission to contact them, the email address. At this stage it's okay to start to sell, but the majority of the relationship is not selling. It's giving great value, building up trust and relationship, but it's ok to sell every now and then.

You always have to keep in mind that you're running a business, not looking for a freebie seeker. You're looking for the customer who's going to buy from you over and over again, and tell other people. One way that you can be doing that is with your emails that you're sending out to people, condition them to click on links in your emails.

Say you've done a great blog post, don't put the whole article in your email - put it on your blog. Put a teaser in your email, something like: "Click here to read it and leave a comment." You're conditioning people so that when they get an email from you saying, "I've got this great program that's for sale. Click this link," they're used to doing it.

> You're conditioning people so that when they get an email from you saying, "Click this link," they're used to doing it.

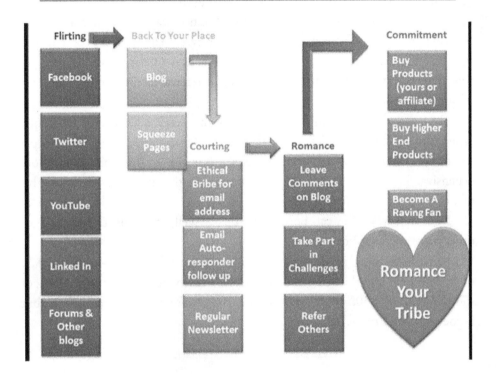

Romance

This is when they're starting to interact with you. How can you encourage this romance to happen?

Blogs are actually a form of social media because people are able to interact through comments. Tell them to leave comments. In your email say, "I made a blog post and I'd love to hear your comments and questions. I'll answer them all."

Give them as many opportunities as you can to interact. You can be running competitions, create a video telling people all about their businesses and put it up on YouTube. Say you'll put a link to the videos on your blog. It's got to be all about them. Challenges like this get people interacting.

Commitment

Now, when we get to the last part, where we actually get the long-term commitment, this is where we really start getting the cash.

There's a few ways that you can do this. The first way is you can start out by referring other people's businesses. I would interview experts and people would then go and purchase products that these experts were offering. I would then get a percentage. It's called an affiliate percentage, a referral fee. It's a significant part of our income in our business.

The other one is to buy your products and services. There's a technique called the inception model or product funnel, where you're giving people the opportunity to buy something cheaper, but also to buy something more expensive. So you start with a low price option, so that they can take a little bit of a risk on you and see if you're worth it.

Next step, you then can be saying, "Okay. Well, if you liked that, I've got other programs that I can be offering you."

You're not going to make your millions from selling an e-book for $20 or $30. Where you do make your money is when you escalate from, "I've got something that's $30," to, "I have another one that's a few hundred dollars, but it goes into a lot more."

You're not going to make your millions from selling an e-book for $20 or $30. You make your money when you escalate from there.

What goes through people's minds is, "Okay. That was a nice little introduction. I want to know more. So I either need a lot more detail or I might need your handholding or I want you to do it for me." That's where the profit lies. You say this is how I can help you and if you want to get a lot more help, well this is going to cost you quite a few thousand dollars, rather than something just being $50.

My advice is to take one action from today. It could be something that might take half an hour to do or something that is going to take you a month to fully implement, but start taking action on one thing today.

Then, drop me an e-mail and tell me what it was. I want to know.

Cydney's Social Wealth Actions Steps:

1. Now it's time for you to start using your social media accounts personally. It's time to start doing some online relationship building. Spend an hour each morning going through one of your social media accounts, with a goal to spending time on each one during the week.

2. Spend some time in particular connecting with key influencers in your LinkedIn network. Follow up with friendly visits, lunches or phone calls if it's appropriate. Build relationships.

3. Also spend time on your Facebook account. This is a network that is frequently changing. Check out the Facebook accounts of the contributors to this book to see what they are doing with their accounts, and connect with us.

4. If you haven't joined Google+, take some time to do so now. Check out our website for articles on how to use Google+ for business. This is a very fast-changing technology, like Facebook.

5. Have you been recording videos to post on YouTube, your blogs, other social media and your websites? If not, now is the time to delegate this job to a team member who enjoys the job and can at least create a series of engaging Animoto.com videos communicating your company messages, values and offers.

CHAPTER 18

MARKETING RAIN MAKER

John Anderson

Founder and CEO, Conversion Masters

Building on his expertise from working in over 30 different industries with over 100 different businesses, John Anderson has been able to engineer documented results like these:

- *Skyrocketing a real estate company's sales by almost $20 million in 3 months*
- *Boosting an event company's revenues by $1.5 million in 12 months*
- *Creating $650,000 in sales for a property education company in a 6-week campaign*

John works with leading companies in the financial services and real estate industries. His time is booked up months in advance and he only takes on new clients by application. He works with companies on a retainer basis, plus equity or a percentage of revenue. Typically clients can expect a massive multiplication of leads and sales within a year.

Many streams make a river

When I work with a new client, if they're mainly communicating with email marketing or direct mail, telesales or whatever they're doing, we add a new communication medium into the mix and that causes a spike in sales.

For example, with one client we added direct mail when they were mainly online. That caused huge results. After all, with email, 10 percent open rates are standard, 20 percent is great, 30 percent is really good and anything above that, you know you're doing something very well.

However, with direct mail you have a much higher chance of actually getting your marketing read because it's *physical*. If you don't have email addresses for past clients, it would be fantastic to make some irresistible offer through direct mail. If you've got a tipping-point product that you know sells well and you send that out by email and you get a great response, that's the time to follow it up with direct mail and potentially telemarketing.

Say there's an accountant that wants to go from being a yearly tax return accountant to being more of a business advisor. He does a sub-launch by email to a few of his clients, inviting them around for a wine and cheese evening where he will launch this new service. He gets a great response, but then he's got another thousand that didn't even open the email. Then he can get his receptionist or bring in a couple of telemarketers to call them all and send out a letter about it. Now, rather than getting the 10 or 20 percent who opened their email, he can get up to 30 or 40 percent reservations to launch the new service.

How to add up to 15 percent to nearly every sale

In the real estate industry, we've just done about $440,000 in sales over the past week for a property education course. We've also done a couple of seven-figure launches in the training and education niche as well.

The cutting-edge of Internet marketing at the moment is the webinar approach. When you're communicating something, the best way to do it is with screenshots, animated videos and webinars because there's nothing that beats a visual demonstration, is there?

Our real estate investment training client has an amazing success rate of 82 percent that bought property and 52 percent who bought two or more. If you can get people to open their manual, that's a win. What we did was demonstrate that information in graphs. We had tables demonstrating how many people took action. A picture tells a thousand words.

Top Internet marketers are making around $70 a lead through the automated webinar system. If you reveal information that is valuable content, then people are going to pay attention. But if you're talking about topics that were hot five years ago, that's not going to grab people's attention. If you want to knock it out of the park, use "never before revealed" content.

Feature whatever is superior about your service and unique about it. Make sure it's solving problems in the customer's world. Show how it's 90 percent faster than its competitors, or whatever it is, it needs to have a uniqueness in the world of your customer.

Feature whatever is superior about your service and unique about it. Make sure it's solving problems in the customer's world.

Email marketing: the secret to an engaged list

The challenge with email is that people are now shielding themselves from emails. The secret is the subject line. Regardless of what list you've got, you can get a higher response by coming up with better subject lines. Frank Kern had one recently: "It's not your fault," which I used with a client. That worked very well in terms of boosting response rates.

Another effective tactic is controversy; if you're dealing with property investors, try: "Property investing crash?" In the Internet marketing space, maybe: "Tell the gurus to go JUMP." That's going to get a lot of people because there's a lot of skepticism about some Internet marketing gurus. That's an example of tapping into a dominant emotion. If you can come up with controversial and anti-conventional type angles, then that's going to bump your response rates.

A twist on conventional logic in your subject line that combines curiosity with a benefit works too. If you had a list of people with a hair loss issue, and you had the subject line: "How a bald barber saved my hair." That's a funny line; you've got to open that, right?

This is gold too: whenever you can go against what everyone else is doing, relevant to your list, just do "the case against." You do "the case against buying silver" and if you're buying silver you've got to read that, or do "the case against video marketing," to a list using video marketing.

Your success is defined by what you say "no" to

We use everything, video, webinars, text messages, telemarketing, Facebook, blog interaction, all in the one campaign. It's full-on and you can make a lot of money out of really hot, direct marketing strategies.

The truth is if anyone ever tells you it's easy, they obviously haven't done it. It's a lot of work. But you can systemize it so it's easier than working in a conventional job. I've been astonished by the amounts of money that can be made, but that doesn't mean there's not a lot of work in it, especially the online marketing. With webinars it's not always necessary to do all that work - because you can do it once and then replay it to new prospects forever.

Develop your PowerPoint, get all the technical issues sorted out with the webinar service you use and get a designer to work with you and get the design right. That's key: robin's egg blues and "credibility colors" like that increase your response rate.

That's key: "credibility colors" increase your response rate.

The top 4 components of any sale

You want to be building an all-star team. You can't really work with people that don't know what they're doing. You want to make sure they're high-quality because things have to get done and done right quickly.

People often approach me with products they want me to create a campaign for and they tell me it'll be a great challenge for me. Here's my idea of a great marketing challenge: a special weight-loss pill that's been proven in 83 double-blind studies that's got 1,000 photo testimonials, huge profit margins and a list of 500,000 overweight people ready to market to. Give me that kind of marketing challenge! That's something I heard from Gary Halbert actually but it really resonated with me. You want to set it up so you're marketing is close to being a slam dunk.

Component #1: Direct mail

There are different approaches to direct mail. If you don't have a top-gun copywriter on your team, it's expensive to do direct mail. Say you're a share-trading service and you may not want to invest $15,000 for a top copywriter to get started, but you do want to get prospects activated.

Use direct mail for just a shy "yes." They don't need to order your new $4,000 trading platform, but you do want them to sign up for a free online tour of it. Use it for something that you're almost guaranteed to get at least some response to and have a P.S. such as: "P.S. If you don't want to take the tour yet, but do want to get a special report or have a video sent to you about it, just email this address."

Make it so easy for people to respond that your investment is very much assured. You're not trying to get the whole sale; you're just taking that first step. If you've got a top-gun copywriter on your team, then you can go a bit further and try to sell. But I'd be more tempted to try to get them registered to a webinar, then sell them in the webinar. If they don't make it to the first webinar, you've got their contact details, you know they're interested and you can follow up.

Obviously you need to work with your legal compliance team for what you can actually send out, but here's an example:

Breakthrough news: I just wanted to keep you up-to-date. The latest government changes to the tax rules could cost you big time. Here's what they are...

I'm on your side. Come to this free tax-planning evening where I'll show you a way to legally and ethically slash your tax bill. I'll also show you a new way of structuring your home loans to save you up to $10,000 a year in interest repayments and much more.

Spaces are limited. This is valued at $X amount. Plus, when you register, you also get a free copy of my new book, Tax Minimization Secrets of the Rich.

That's the sort of benefit driven copy you want to run with.

Component #2: Telemarketing

There are two different ways that we can look at telemarketing. One is, using the financial planner example, bringing in a couple of commerce students that want to learn more about the financial planning industry. We get them calling up our clients in the evenings and booking them into free tax-planning sessions.

Then there's another approach we use: find a star performer who's going to grow the business, who is prepared to start off on a low base and get 20 percent of all the commissions that they earn me. They network with the right people and build relationships and position you as *the* financial planner to see. They're very consultative, sending out the latest reports about the stock market, the latest reports about property and the latest tax planner reports from the tax authorities. We're building a relationship with these people; we're in regular dialogue.

They create business for the financial planner through these highly qualified, high net worth individuals.

Let's now talk about what to actually focus on in your marketing, if you can find the urgent problem and desire of your market. It's about getting into that conversation and the dominant emotion. Play against what's being done to death and offer new information. Provide proof; do a demonstration. In terms of direct marketing, probably nothing has moved more product than infomercials, which have moved billions of dollars of products. That's because they allow you to visually demonstrate your product. Do the same; find a way to visually demonstrate your product.

Whenever you can have a premium service, there will be people who may want a concierge service. You can charge more, and they get a done-for-you service, a "hard-back" edition. Having two levels is perfect. Say you're someone that likes the fine things in life. If you sign up for something, you're going to want the top level. But not everyone can do that, or wants to, so you have another level for them. For some people, it's almost a religion for them to choose the top level, whereas some people are just trying to get by and they just want to get on board but they can't afford the premium offer.

Always have different levels of service. Trial offers can be the best thing ever, for example, "Send no money now. We'll bill you. We won't bill you for 30 days. If you don't like it just send it back and you won't have to pay a cent."

Component #3: Chameleon marketing

Make your marketing not look like marketing and you'll get a much better response. Rather than having a sales letter look like a sales letter with a headline at the top and paragraphs and bullet points and a guarantee, design it like magazine! You put the headlines on the front and then put in articles and some really valuable tips, maybe you've got 40 or 50 percent content. Then build up to the offer at the end. That's the way a "magalog" works.

Make your marketing not look like marketing
and you'll get a much better response.

Component #4: The big direct marketing secret

Lately, we've made around $100,000 a day over the past 4 days, which has been pretty amazing, in one product launch. We launched a supplement range and made the client about $120,000 a day in consistent income. Other campaigns have made over $1 million in income this year.

Really, what it all comes down to is a powerful, value-based product launch. By that I mean sending out hot content-based videos, webinars, special reports that just completely electrify your market because the content's so good, it's so valuable. Build up the relationship; build up the trust and the credibility. Then launch the product with an incredible offer, and you've followed all these steps correctly you should make good money.

Cydney's Social Wealth Action Steps:

1. By now you should have:
    a. Your social media accounts set up; LinkedIn, Facebook, Youtube, Twitter, Google+ and others you might think appropriate
    b. Articles and press releases being released and posted regularly
    c. Reviewed and revised copy messaging and marketing
    d. Compelling and appropriate branding
    e. Some good causes that are organizing reciprocal campaigns with you
    f. Attendance and exposure at live and community events
2. John recommends that you add some other methods of automation and communication into the mix, such as a high-value telemarketing campaign to talk to your prospects in a positive way. Make sure you are offering great value to your customers.

3. Create an informative webinar or educational video and invite your network to view it at a certain date and time. Consider automating the replays of the information, as this can be of great value to those not able to make the live event.

4. Create an inspired email marketing campaign, particularly if you have something new and exciting to launch. A book, for instance, gives you a great opportunity to have a launch and gift your clients and prospects with something of perceived high value.

5. Consider a direct mail campaign and whether or not a magalog or sales brochure in the form of a magazine would be viable and add a profitable boost to your bottom line.

CHAPTER 19

THINK BIGGER WITH DIGITAL MARKETING

Pam & Steve Brossman

Magnetic Digital Marketing

Pam Brossman is the CEO of SocialMediaWoman.com and publisher of the international online magazine, Social Media Woman. She has over 25 years in corporate communications and, together with her husband Steve Brossman, founded Magnetic Digital Marketing. Their vision is to help women all around the world grow their business and their brand effectively using the power of video, digital marketing and social media marketing.

More beach time

When we had our son later in life, we decided that he deserved our time and it didn't sit well with me that Steve seemed to be hanging out at the beach having coffees as an entrepreneur. I was in an office and he was hanging out at the beach. I decided that a lifestyle change was in order; and wanted to become an entrepreneur. Now I'm an author and international speaker and, with Steve, regularly speak on the topic of digital marketing on stages around the world.

Most people have experience in so many different areas that they could be sharing on a global scale, but they're either doing presentations face-to-face or they're coaching face-to-face and they're limiting the possibilities by not thinking digital. We want to show you how you can have a bigger reach–your marketplace is probably 300 times what you thought it could be–how you can increase your return on investment and open up the door to so many opportunities that you never even thought of by using the power of digital marketing, digital branding, digital product creation and just starting to think bigger, through video and online information marketing.

What you need to make videos

One of the key reasons people hold back is they think doing videos is really expensive. They are thinking old school; that you have to get a professional TV camera person to come and shoot your video, then pay them to edit it and then pay for it all to be put on. That's a thing of the past. In fact, if anybody is hurting at the moment it's the TV stations and the videographers who used to get paid big money. Now, people are learning to do it themselves.

Start out with a video camera that's under $200 and a microphone for around $40. Audio is really important; people will turn off if the audio quality is really bad. Those of you who want to get a little bit more professional and start green screening, that's between $500 and $800. A green screen allows you to digitally place different backgrounds in your video. It's a one-off expense. Once you've spent that to set up, then you get your money back so quickly that the expense is minimal.

If you just want to start out and maybe do some video blogging, it's as simple as using your webcam or your laptop. Most of them have a built in webcam these days, but I do highly recommend if you want good quality to get an HD webcam.

To start doing videos, all you need is a camera, microphone, and editing software. If you have Microsoft on your computer you can use Microsoft Windows Movie Maker, that's one. Windows Movie Maker comes with Microsoft and if you are on a Mac then iMovie comes with the package, very basic and easy to use, and that's all you need. There are also some online editors you can use if you want, too. YouTube even has its own editor so you can edit videos once you have posted to YouTube. So there is no excuse; editing is not complicated.

Presenting your video

The number one pain people have about using video is: "Do I have to be in front of the camera?" That used to be me, says Pam. I went six months without being in front of the camera. I kept telling Steve to do it, "you shoot the video, I don't want to be in front of the camera". I was very uncomfortable seeing myself on camera, so what I used was Powerpoint videos and images my first six months.

But I realized that the engagement of people actually getting to know me, the like and trust factor, I couldn't get with a Powerpoint. So I got over my fear of being in front of the camera and as soon as I started to do face-to-camera videos, my business took off. I started getting people saying, "Oh, so that's who you are Pam! I've been following you for two, three, four months now, and it's so lovely to meet you in person!"

So I got over my fear of being in front of the camera and as soon as I started to do face-to-camera videos, my business took off.

I had a database of people in the U.S. who had never met me before. So to be able to feel like they knew me by watching me on video opened up huge opportunities and doors. If you're really nervous, you can get started and just do screen capture or Powerpoints, but eventually, just start by doing a webcam and getting comfortable even with having one on your blog.

Steve says, "It's what people love about you anyway. People don't run away when you walk into a room do they?" So all you're really doing is exactly what you do in day-to-day life at a coffee shop or when you walk into a party or barbeque. All you're doing is the same sort of conversation on camera.

Do's & don'ts with video

When doing your video, don't read from a script unless you are gifted with the ability to read like a newsreader. We never read from a script. I find it really hard to put your personality into a video when you read from a script. So what you need to do is have three key points that you want to make and put them on a wall in front of you. Use those bullet points to guide you through the three things you need to cover in that video, then underneath that, just have your closing and call to action. You do not have to cover everything in that one video.

A great way to start is to say, "Hi, this is Pam Brossman here and in this short video, I'm going to share with you three things that you must know before doing your blog to make sure that people watch it." So they know exactly what they're going to learn. They know it's a short video, they know I'm only covering three points. Then, I go through the points and say "If you want more, if you enjoyed this, please share it with your friends." My call to action would be to leave a comment and have my Facebook comment box there. They leave a comment and it gets shared on Facebook. If it is on YouTube, then your call to action would be to subscribe to your channel, leave a comment, share with your friends and/or click on the link below to get a free report. But always send them to your website.

How often should you do videos?

This is a question we get asked a lot from offline businesses because obviously businesses have to go about their day-to-day jobs and they see that doing videos is just another thing that they have to add to their list.

For content, the main thing we teach people to do is frequently asked questions. What are the ten most frequently asked questions you get asked every day on the phone or face-to-face in your store? Then, what are the ten questions that people should be asking that they don't ask, that they really need to know about your product, service or business? Another good tip and to do a keyword search using the free keyword tool: type in your keyword and do a video on the top ten keywords for your niche that show up there. That way you know people are already searching for that topic.

Shoot them all in one day and roll them out. Once a week, once every two weeks, once a month. Have all of them backlinking to your business, because every video you put out there is a little bit of real estate that people find online and that sends them back to your business.

Every video you put out there is a little bit of real estate that people find online and that sends them back to your business.

The other thing you can do once a week or once a month is your video newsletter. Do what works for you. If you're already doing a newsletter, add a video to it and just shoot it once-a-month. Steve and I have a video day and we shoot the next four weeks or the next two months of videos in one day. Then we send them to be edited, and we get our virtual assistant to upload them for us. If you want to do it the lazy man's way, you can do the webcam, where you just sit in front of your webcam. Recording takes you three minutes, upload and there you go. There's no perfect recipe; it depends on your business. For us, the more videos we have out there, the more traction we're getting back to our business.

The other tip is you can repurpose that one video. You can shoot that video, put it on YouTube, then put it in your newsletter, your blog post and put it out there on social media and get all of this traction, just from one video. You don't have to shoot lots of videos, but to get a lot of traction, I would be doing a minimum of two a month, four is even better. One a week and you will start seeing results.

What kind of videos work for business?

Video emails are very popular. We've noticed that the open rates with emails that have a video thumbnail that takes you back to the website are much higher than emails that don't. People are getting inundated with emails and spam, so it's getting harder and harder to stand out in the crowd. So video email is one, video newsletters are the other.

We have had huge success with video newsletters, but we have just moved across to video blogging and the reason why is that Google loves blogs. We're getting traction a lot faster from our blog posts than we did from the video page. Google loves video blogs, video proposals and video signatures.

Here's an example of a video signature. Say you worked in a gym and you were an instructor. You were sending out emails to get some new leads and you had a video at the bottom. People click on that video, and it would go to your web page and say, "Hi, my name is Mike, and I'm really excited that you popped in. I know that you're probably thinking, Oh, I've got to lose a little bit of weight. Well, I would love to help you do that and make it really, really easy and really, really fun. If you want to chat to me about it just contact me below." Then, a contact form. How much more personal is that? Imagine if you had a video that made a potential customer think, "Oh wow! He seems really nice!" Do you think it would make a difference?

What's working the best at the moment is giving away video tutorials, adding value to the client. Give away maybe four or five tutorials, with one sales video. They can be short. It could be something like "I just found this new tool today. It's really cool and this is how you use it." Our market loves it. Then, we upsell to them because we're affiliates. They don't mind because we have shown them how it can add value to their business, how to implement it and then the decision is theirs. You can't do that in just an email.

How videos help in finding your business

Does a video help you get on page one of the search engines? Most definitely! That's one of the number one reasons why I got started in the first place. You do have to understand video SEO, but that's very, very simple to do. You cannot just put a video up and they'll find it, that's not how it works. Make sure you're uploading to YouTube, that you have your keywords in your headline, your keywords in your description and also have keywords in your tags.

> Does a video help you get on page one
> of the search engines? Most definitely!

You can also get on page one of YouTube. People underestimate the value of that. More and more people are hanging out there, and it's the second most searched engine online now. Getting page one on YouTube is a lot easier than getting on page one of Google. These days people can sort how they want their views to be seen in the search engines. They can say I only want local stuff or I only want stuff that I have viewed recently. So because you're changing all of the search results, what I see on my page one may not be the same thing on your page one. So it's getting harder and harder for people to see the same view on search engines. But when you're on YouTube, everybody sees the same thing. So if you're on page one of YouTube, you're on page one.

> YouTube is the second most searched engine
> online–and getting on page one on YouTube is a
> lot easier than getting on page one of Google.

Videos are also a very important way to drive traffic back to your business and position your brand. As you can imagine, if you've typed in the words "Tiny's Restaurant" and you've got five or six links dominating that page, where do you think people's eyes go? They don't go to those little links. They go straight to the video. People will want to see it. "Wow, look at that testimonial! Look at the food. Look at the layout." You can't get that with a link.

Cydney's Social Wealth Action steps:

1. Create a list of the 10 most frequently asked questions by your client base and prospects.
2. Prepare the answers to these questions.
3. Create a list of the top 10 questions that people should be asking about your niche and prepare the answers to those questions.
4. Do some keyword research on the top 10 topics being searched online in your areas of expertise that you have solutions for.
5. Create a collection of simple videos discussing these topics, either in Powerpoint presentation form, face-to-camera form, interview format, or animated video, such as Animoto.com. Post your videos on your sites, blogs, social media accounts and video channels.

CHAPTER 20

LINKEDIN AND THE NEW RULES OF BUSINESS CONNECTION

Iggy Pintado

Author, Speaker and Connector

Iggy Pintado is a professional speaker and author of Connection Generation as well as the Director of Solutions and Marketing at UXC Connect. He is an experienced business leader, executive and connector. Over 22 years, he has held professional, management and executive positions in marketing, sales, channels, operations and online management at both IBM and Telstra. An accomplished business leader, he is an internationally-recognized Connection Technology Practitioner. As a super-connected networker on LinkedIn, Facebook, Twitter and Foursquare he has earned his place in the top 25 list of the most connected business networkers in Australia.

Exponential networking

I saw the power of networking very early in my career. There are tips and tricks in terms of how to not only network well, which a lot of people know how to do, but to leverage it for business. A lot of people think that social media is something all new and exciting, but I think it's around this concept of connectivity and connection and being able to harness that power on a platform like social media where you get the most benefit.

What I want to take you through is the power of connecting for business and specifically looking at a business platform like LinkedIn and how to leverage that for corporate networking to actually get some promotional value out of it.

We're moving from a *transactional* economy to a *relational* economy. People don't just buy products anymore. So your brand needs to be something that people relate to. It has to be accessible and engaging. There must be a connection between your prospects and customers and the products and services you're offering that goes beyond the transaction. How do you become connected? What are the key elements? The basics are still there. The things that we used to do ages ago are still there. You still need business cards, some sort of collateral or merchandising to promote your business. You still need to be listed so that people can find you. It may not be the White or Yellow Pages; the world's changed. People remember names or they search by product or service.

You've got to have some sort of merchandising, promotional items a product or service to sell. You've got to be found and your Google listing is critical. If you're not there, you don't exist in the minds of your customers or your prospects. A website so people can find you is a competitive necessity, like an electronic brochure. It tells people who you are. I also strongly recommend to any business that they have a blog, a site that says to people what they think.

If you're not on Google, you don't exist in the
minds of your customers or your prospects.

For example, if you're in the environmental business, people don't just want to know about your products and services. They want to know what you think about things like climate change and carbon tax.

Once you've got a website and a blog, get social, go on the various platforms of social media: LinkedIn, Twitter, Facebook, YouTube, Skype, SlideShare and even eBay if you're selling products. When you're listed on each of these sites, it lists you on Google. So having a website and a blog is two presences; LinkedIn,

Facebook and eBay mean you have multiple presences and a better chance of being found on Google.

If your customers are only on Twitter, then you need to be found on Twitter. If they're on YouTube, you need to be found on YouTube. If your customers are on Facebook, be on Facebook.

LinkedIn

Facebook and Twitter are places where brands want to talk about experiences and get opportunities. But to me, LinkedIn is really where you find your next customers, where you can profile them, look at your target market and engage them in a meaningful way.

What is LinkedIn? It is the world's largest audience of affluent influential professionals. There are now over 135 million members: 55 million in the U.S. and the rest are outside of the US, mainly in Europe. Audience profile is about 50/50 male to female. The average income is $91,566 annually and the average age is 45 years old. They have college and post-grad degrees. Senior management is well represented as well as middle management, people who influence and make business purchases. These are people who are online every day who look for posts and product reviews on a regular basis. All this information is LinkedIn's data. Just look at "About LinkedIn."

It took 494 days to reach the first million members and on average a new member joins every second, so about a million people join every twelve days. More people who are entering the workforce are discovering the power of LinkedIn. The database is continually expanding as people start to discover the real value of it. You get Fortune 500 companies as members, people who are fairly senior in organizations.

How to use LinkedIn

Make sure you are perceived online the way you want to be perceived offline. This is your electronic business card. Spend time on your profile. I don't actually carry or keep business cards. When I go to social or business functions, I encourage people to invite me on LinkedIn and I use LinkedIn as my CRM (Customer Relationship Management system). I pay an extra $20 a month to get special access to LinkedIn that allows me to tag my connections by last name, company name, location, industry and activity. I can add and remove them.

I don't actually carry business cards. I
encourage people to invite me on LinkedIn.

With LinkedIn connections, you can export them to a .csv or Excel file. By export, I mean you can export first name, last name and email address. That means you can put them into an email engine. If I invited you and you accepted my invitation or you invited me and I accepted the invitation, then it's opting into my network, which means that I can email you as long as I don't spam you.

I can actually use it as a CRM. I can add phone numbers, addresses, birthdays and other information, and have that available on my own PC. You can download that data as well. I'm also notified on an annual basis whenever my connections change jobs. This is of particular value to people who have databases. If you have a business card and you change jobs in six months' time, most of the information on that business card is probably irrelevant.

It's up to the individual whose profile you have to change their details. So the data is always dynamic and relevant. I also use it for mobile; my database isn't on my computer or iPad, it's on a device that I can access easily.

The new four "Ps" of online connection

I want to cover the commercial uses of what I call the new four "Ps" of online connection: Purpose, Profiling, Patience and Persistence.

Purpose: Don't go onto Facebook, LinkedIn or Twitter just because everybody else has. Think about what you're trying to do. Are you trying to profile your business? Trying to research companies? Using it for sales prospecting? Are you using LinkedIn specifically to showcase your products? (There's a product capability on LinkedIn.) Are you trying to target your audience or buy some extra capabilities so that you can do some mapping around industry, number of employees, specific locations? Are you using it to engage your customers through things like Groups and Answers?

Understand what you are trying to do with it so you cannot only meet your expectations, but get return on the investment of time it will take you to learn enough to be involved.

You've got to participate, put yourself
out there and ask people to engage.

Profile: It's important to make sure that your profile is built properly and that it does reflect who you are. I took a screen shot of Barack Obama when he was a candidate for the U.S. Presidency. He has his past, his education, the number of connections. In the last few days of the election, he was the 14th most connected person on LinkedIn. He was using LinkedIn and engaging with others as a way to get corporate America to help with his campaign.

Your online profile is your personal brand; it reflects the brand you represent.

Participation: You've got to participate, put yourself out there and ask people to engage. Ask questions, get involved in groups and socialize. Bill Gates joined LinkedIn to put this up on LinkedIn's Answers forum: "How can we do more to encourage young people to pursue careers in science and technology?" Within two months, he got 3,566 answers.

Accelerated wealth secret:
The average income of people on LinkedIn is around $90,000, and they are very educated.

Remember the profile of people on LinkedIn is 45 years old, average income around $90,000 and very educated. So this is an informed audience. Bill Gates specifically asked on this platform because he wanted to get the best views. I'm assuming that his staff went through these 3,566 answers and looked for the great ideas. This research cost him nothing, a simple post on a website. This is the best example of crowd sourcing that I have seen relative to business, technology and career management.

Persistence: You have to be persistent, build a strategy and engage with people. Hewlett Packard used LinkedIn as a way to create new opportunities for their brand, to engage commercially with their clients. They encourage business professionals to recommend HP products and services and built a critical mass of recommendations. Some of the results of their campaigning: 2,000 product recommendations, 20,000 new followers on their page and 500,000 viral updates about HP's products and services.

They kept at it and kept at it. This didn't happen overnight.

Cydney's social wealth action steps:

1. If you don't already have one, set up Skype, Slideshare and eBay accounts for your business and yourself personally, as a representative of your business. Post some of your great Powerpoints on topics relating to your market and set up a regular sale of e-books and products that promote your business, following eBay guidelines.
2. Think about your purpose with these accounts and your LinkedIn account. What are your end goals?
3. Participate in and encourage conversations that will engage your network, but also help you learn more about your market.
4. Set up your account on LinkedIn like a CRM system. Organize your contacts into groups that will enable you to send posts more effectively.
5. Spend some time going through communities on LinkedIn and join in and/or start some of your own.

CHAPTER 21

CONNECTED LIFESTYLE DESIGN

Dr. Joanna Martin

Founder and CEO, Shift Lifestyle International

I wrote this from an extensive interview with Dr Joanna Martin, a sought-after educator who has taught over 55,000 people on 3 continents. She is one of the world's most successful and inspirational speakers, having taken her own business from standstill to seven figures and two countries in twelve months. She is widely regarded as a lifestyle design specialist. She started her working life as a medical doctor, then was trained at the prestigious Actors Centre Australia. It is her odd mix of first class honors in medicine combined with her irreverent performer's attitude that brings a quirky and feminine approach to an industry dominated by men. Joanna's corporate clients include Australia's ANZ Bank, Fairfax Publishing and eBay, and her students include successful seven-figure speakers and numerous publicly recognized clients. She is now based between London and Melbourne. With her partner, Greg, through their business, Shift Lifestyle, they provide strategy and support for business owners who want to join the "Lifestyle Revolution."

An extraordinary life

I've never wanted to accept anything less than extraordinary from my life. I've always been that way and whenever anything is starting to be less than extraordinary, I shake it all up again. That's how I coined the phrase "Lifestyle Shift."

We have two very successful businesses: one in the U.K. and one in Australia. We have an incredible team that I am so grateful for. This is something we have created very deliberately. I think that fabulous lifestyles are rarely things that occur by chance. It's something that takes some deliberate setting up. When was the last time you had a big dream about where you wanted your lifestyle to be? And are you there? Have you've got the kind of money that you want to be making?

There have been times where that wasn't the case for me. My first lifestyle shift was when I was working as a medical doctor and I lost a very dear patient to breast cancer. I'm really talking about a quantum shift in the way you operate day to day. That's what occurred for me. I went off to drama school after that. I thought, "This is not what I'm meant to be doing." Have the courage to go after something you had given up on, whether that's growing a business, or making a difference in a new way, or having the relationship of your dreams. Whatever it is, have the courage to go after it.

Have the courage to go after something you had given up on, whether it's growing a business or making a difference or having the relationship of your dreams. Whatever it is, go after it.

I believe that your heart's desire is what the universe wants for you. If you want it, you're meant to have it. My heart said, "Go to drama school," and that's what I did. How do you know if you're ready for a lifestyle shift? You might be feeling a bit frantic, or like an area of your life is not working out. You might be getting great results, say, with your family but your business just isn't where you want it to be, or you're getting great results with your business but the last time you had a fulfilling relationship was 20 years ago.

If you're aligned with your soul purpose, it's always working out, even if it feels crazy. I see really successful people, their businesses are great, they're in great marriages, they've got great kids, they're making good money, but they're just like, "Hmm, is this it?" It's just a feeling of something missing. Any of those things might be triggers that you're ready for a lifestyle shift. I'll tell you now, you will have a shift because the universe will make it to happen for you, whether you want it or not. Every single day we get to choose to grow or we have growth forced upon us.

Every single day we get to choose to
grow or we have growth forced upon us.

It's much more elegant when we make the choice to be connected. I've got this crazy belief that our soul provides us with a river of momentum towards our destiny, if we just open up to it. If you're not connected, you can only ever create results with your willpower.

Personality

The first thing we need to connect with is our personality strengths. I use the Wealth Dynamics profiling tool. There's a lot of profiling tools and they're all fantastic. For business people, I believe this one is the most useful. There are the eight different wealth dynamics profiles: Creator, Star, Supporter, Deal Maker, Trader, Accumulator, Lord and Mechanic. Interestingly, in every industry, there's a role for every profile. Reconnect to your personality strengths–what you are naturally good at, what sets you on fire–and make sure that whatever fast millionaire formula you're choosing, it is something which allows you to demonstrate and live from those strengths. I can't tell you how many Internet marketing packages I bought before I discovered I hate sitting in front of a computer. I'm a people person.

Get connected to yourself (your strengths), your source (the river that's going to flow through you, to provide you with the energy you need every step of the way) and your purpose (the direction that you want to be heading). If you're connected to all of those things, then it cannot feel like hard work. Then you're going to be starting to get ready to choose the right strategy. You're not ready yet, but you're primed. To create your ultimate lifestyle you need to create a connection habit. Something you do regularly and daily.

When love isn't enough

There was a time in my life where I was doing something I absolutely loved. For three years, I got to travel the world. I was on stage in front of thousands of people. I wasn't acting, I was speaking and I was teaching, but I was achieving these visions that I'd had when I was young and I was loving what I was doing. It was fantastic. But then on my 30th birthday, I was in London, I loved the people I was working with, but it's not the same as being with your family and your loved ones. I thought, I don't like this life anymore. I cannot stand on stage today and say, "These tools will help you have the lifestyle of your dreams," because right now, I don't have the lifestyle of my dreams. I nearly burned out doing what I loved. Be aware that if you're doing what you love already, you're most at risk of this.

After nine months of doing nothing, I got bored. Greg and I decided we'd start a business. But we were going to do it right. Do you know what the interesting thing was? Every time we tried to set a goal, we veered off on a conversation about what we *wouldn't* do. We ended up discussing something much bigger than goals, something I now refer to as lifestyle priorities. We wanted to create the ultimate lifestyle business. I wanted to be doing what I love, but I did not want to compromise my lifestyle.

There's this millionaire myth–this is something that Timothy Ferriss talks about in his awesome book *The 4-Hour Workweek*, which I highly recommend– you don't need a million dollars to live a millionaire lifestyle. I was living a millionaire lifestyle long before I was a millionaire and I was still investing in savings for my future at the same time.

Clarity

The second shift that Greg and I realized after reconnecting was this clarity. Once connection is established, it's now time to start designing your lifestyle from this place of flow that we were talking about. The order that we do it is to first define your lifestyle priorities and then second, define your business criteria, because number three is then selecting the business vehicle. You want to start with clarity on what you want your lifestyle to look like. Before you choose any fast millionaire formula, what do you want your daily life to consist of? What do you want your lifestyle to look like? These become your lifestyle priorities.

I don't know what your lifestyle priorities are–it might be adventure, serenity or peace. Once you've got that, then it's time to define the business criteria, but not which vehicle you're choosing yet. Define which criteria your business must fulfill in order to provide for that lifestyle. Then, once you've done that, you create your elegant business model and you choose what I refer to as a freedom vehicle. Now you're ready to choose your fast millionaire formula, the right one for you. When you've gone through that process, it'll give you so much more clarity in being able to choose one. Something aligned with your purpose, that leverages your personality strengths, what you're passionate about, your talents, and it fulfills those lifestyle business criteria we've talked about. Any business model that means that you get paid an hourly wage is never going to give you freedom because if you stop working, you stop making money. Ultimately, you want to create some vehicle that allows you to massively leverage your hourly rate or better still, it makes money without you.

> Any business that means you get paid an hourly
> wage is never going to give you freedom because
> if you stop working, you stop making money.

Accelerated wealth secret:
Design your elegant business model™

There are all sorts of business vehicles or elegant business models (EBM) that will provide for that–millions of them. Anything can provide for your lifestyle, but remember it's got to be that way around; you don't just go and choose this one because someone tells you that's going to make you a lot of money. We chose our Shift Speaker Training business. Because we'd done this from a place of flow, we'd gone through this process of making sure the business served our lifestyle, rather than took away from it, some of the results we got, to this day, shock even Greg and me. Within 12 months, we were getting some pretty incredible results. I do my speaking and I sell this product and we deliver it online month in, month out. In December 2008–we'd only been in business about 8 months then–we were doing $8,000 a month from that product. Then when I went out and did events, we did $256,000 in May 2009 just from the event-related income. Yes, I studied a lot. I learned about marketing and did a lot of personal development. I think you've got to do both of those things; you've got to have your psychology in place and you've got to be learning. Then when you get started on the right thing at the right time for you, for what's going on in the world and what the market wants, then this kind of magic can happen very, very easily, which is really exciting.

We give a significant percentage of our profits straight to The Hunger Project. It's incredibly inspiring. We're getting some great results. What they do is incredible, and the way they do it. They don't put money into a community until the mindset of the community has shifted sufficiently that they own their own solutions.

Community

The third shift is community. If you want to have an incredible life, you need to have an incredible community. There are three elements to a great community: the first is your peers and your network. I think part of your millionaire formula has to be hanging out with the right people. Then I think the second component is having the right mentors and advisers. But there are two different types of mentors and advisers to be aware of and you don't want to confuse them: the first one is a strategy adviser, a strategy mentor. When you've got your lifestyle priorities in place, you're clear on what criteria your business needs to fulfill, and you've selected the business vehicle that's right for you. Find a strategy adviser who has achieved results with that strategy.

Then there's another kind of adviser you need, more of a coach. That's what I see myself as. Lifestyle design is not about helping someone to become a good Internet marketer. Lifestyle design is about being a soul coach, a soul mentor; asking the right questions to help someone create and design their life the way they want it. Sometimes you have more than one strategy mentor. You might have a financial adviser as well.

Your freedom team

Then the third element of your community is what I call your "freedom team." In the old days, you would have said this is your staff, but it's more than your staff. Creating a great team is where what you provide is so much more than the money that you pay. It does mean that eventually, when you can, you do pay great money, because it's fun to help people provide for their lifestyle.

We created the purpose of Shift together. It originally started with my life purpose, but we massaged it and tweaked it with the team. If you have a big enough vision that people are really excited by and they want to be a part of it, you will attract people who want to contribute to something amazing, not just people who want a paycheck. You want to attract your freedom team and be very conscious about who you're bringing on to support you every step of the way. Honestly, you will never have a great lifestyle business when it's just you.

Overcome the capability trap so that you don't do the things you shouldn't be doing. Give them to someone who does them better than you. Then make sure you set up this command center so that every day you're spending energy only on the things that move you towards your lifestyle. I have this incredible lifestyle because once a year I do this 12-month planning. We break it right down, then once a month I do my monthly planning and once a week I do my weekly planning, and daily I do my daily planning. Then when I have a holiday, I don't do any of it.

Overcome the capability trap so that you don't do the things you shouldn't be doing. Give them to someone who does them better than you.

If what we've been talking about today resonates and people want to go through the program to get that level of clarity before they start choosing what they should be doing or what direction they should be taking their business, or even if they're in the right business to start with, then I recommend the Lifestyle Shift Accelerator Program. This is an eight-week transformational home-study program. It's something you can do from home, focusing on the 20 percent of your activities that are going to get you 80 percent of your results towards that lifestyle. You can have lifetime access to the program, which is eight video trainings, taking you step by step through everything in much more detail, plus lots of guided mediations to help you get clear on the different pieces as we go. There are audios that you can put on your iPod and all of the transcriptions and workbooks that go with it. We will include a wealth dynamics profile for you. I think it's really important that you understand your wealth dynamics profile.

I hope that if my mission for an extraordinary life can inspire others to live an extraordinary life as well, then I think that's a life well served. I believe if all of us were living our purpose and if all of us were making the difference that we were put on this planet to make, then there couldn't be world hunger, there couldn't be war, they're couldn't be abused children, or any of that stuff. If every person was living in alignment with their heart's desire, it just couldn't occur. That's what I really want to do: inspire people to step up and live their extraordinary life.

Cydney's social wealth action steps:

1. Get clear on your personality strengths and weaknesses. Joanna recommends the Wealth Dynamics profiling tool; you'll find this and other personality profiling resources at www.MillionairesAcademy. com. Answer the questionnaire and get an overview.

2. Have your core team also take the profile so that you know the strengths and weaknesses in your management team and can allocate responsibilities accordingly.

3. Get clarity on your life purpose and ideal lifestyle.

4. Get clear on your freedom vehicle, or business type.

5. Design your own elegant business model.

GROW

It is a paradoxical but profoundly true and important principle of life that the most likely way to reach a goal is to be aiming not at that goal itself but at some more ambitious goal beyond it.

– Arnold Toynbee

CHAPTER 22

LEVERAGED EXPANSION

Domenic Carosa

Founder and CEO,
Dominet Digital Corp.

Domenic is the Founder and CEO of Dominet Digital Corporation, a boutique investment and consulting group with a focus on digital innovation and investments. The success of any "upstart" business is based on having the right ingredients across strategy, sales, marketing, financial and operations. Domenic co-founded what was to become Destra Corporation in 1993 when he was in his late teens. He listed it on the Australian Stock Exchange in May 2000, making him the youngest CEO of a publicly listed company in Australia at that time. Under his direction, Destra branched out from its core web hosting and communications business to become one of Australia's largest independent media and entertainment companies. The company had annualized revenues of over $100 million in 2008.

Domenic is currently the Chairman of the Internet Industry Association and Chairman of the Board of Future Capital Development Fund Limited, which is a development fund aimed at assisting in the development of emergent companies.

Business from the bedroom

I started in my bedroom importing video games and accessories. I got involved in software in 1994 or 1995. I got involved in Internet marketing in 1995 or 1996, so was on the Internet well before it was fashionable.

Typically, an entrepreneur knows a little bit about a whole bunch, isn't a master of anything, but is smart enough to realize that. What they are actually really good at is identifying really smart people and bringing them together, focused towards a common vision, to achieve big things. They hire the best finance, marketing, the best salespeople they can to work around them.

We saw the whole dot-com thing starting to take shape and we launched MP3.com.au in the late 1990s. We saw that the music industry was starting to change, so we registered the domain and launched Australia's first independent digital download service.

We had gone from 20-odd people pre-listing to about 50–60 people post-listing. Our core revenue streams were going to come from the sale of digital music and online advertising.

Caught out

After the dot-com crash, the Australian online advertising market collapsed. It was all the dot-coms spending money, and they were going broke. These days, it's the fastest growing segment. Our model also depended upon the record companies providing use licenses to content, but in 2001 they decided they weren't going to do anything when it came to digital music.

We were dependent on content sales and online advertising; we didn't expect both things to collapse. Stuff happens in life and business. As the CEO of Intel used to say, "Only the paranoid survive." I adopt that philosophy because you never know what is around the corner.

Rebuild

From 2001 to 2005, we refocused our attention to web hosting and built the second largest virtual web host in the country. In 2005, we sold that and the domain name and comm business for $25 million. We went back to our roots, which were digital media. Over time, we built the largest independent media and entertainment company in Australia. From that perspective, it was all going really well. In my last half-year as CEO, we delivered a $50 million red line and a $6 million EBIT profit. That's in six months, so annualized it was over $100 million of revenue flowing through.

In my last half-year as CEO, we delivered a
$50 million red line and a $6 million EBIT profit.

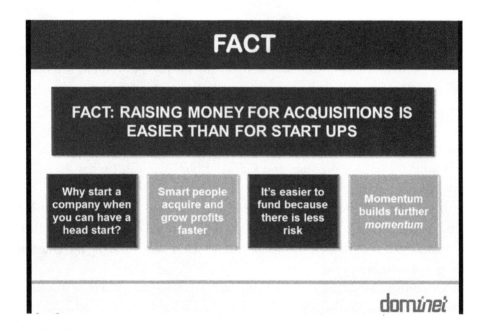

What I do these days is look for and invest in interesting Internet companies. We've been working with the founders, the entrepreneurs and helping grow them, and then at the right point in time, we get involved in a trade sale. Effectively, on a daily basis, we have people contacting us wanting capital for their Internet companies. That's all we do. There are other funds that focus on different sectors, but our core expertise, understanding and what we really love are Internet-related.

What we look for when evaluating a company

I get information memorandums (IMs), business plans, but what I do first is go to the exec summary and have a quick read of that one page. I ask myself, "Is there a gap in the market?"

Then I look at who the people are, who the management team is. If it's a management team I've never heard about or they don't have what I believe are the right kinds of expertise or experience, I will then look at who the Board of

Directors are, who the Board of Advisers are. I want to know who is mentoring these executives.

"Domisms" – Success tips

I want to share a couple of tools that I like to use:

I use "what you can measure, you can change." This is a really interesting tool by Shirlaws called "Red, Blue and Black." I'll just go through it quickly. Red is back office, IT, all the stuff that, typically, as an entrepreneur you hate doing but that has to be done. Blue is the sales, the cash flow, the marketing, the stuff that brings in the deals. Black is the joint ventures, the capital raisings, the acquisitions, the stuff that will add significant value to your business.

I ask a lot of entrepreneurs and CEOs of our investees, "What does your Red, Blue and Black look like? "

If you are spending too much time in the Red, find people to do the Red stuff. As the business grows, bring in the right people to do the Blue, then over time, your core focus is the black stuff, which makes those big incremental changes to your business.

Sometimes people ask me, "If I don't have mentor or a Board of Advisers, how do I go about finding them?"

The question I ask is: "Who are you as an individual?" If you can get an understanding or insight into who you are, you are better able to bring someone on board who is complimentary to you.

Finding the right people for your team

A big chunk of the people we hire are actually from our networks. I use social networks: LinkedIn, Facebook, my email list. It's usually one or two degrees of separation. Occasionally, we will use things like Seek.com in order to hire people.

First, I look for cultural fit, the right kind of personality type. Second, what I look for is do they have the skills? My personal view is you cannot teach someone passion and persistence, but you can teach someone some sales skills, some product skills, some technical skills. So I look for people with the right kind of personality, then we focus on the skills required to perform that particular function.

"Hire slow, fire fast" is something that it's taken me a little while to learn. There's a saying: "The occasional firing in any organization is positive." Those at the bottom end of the performance spectrum lift their performance on the fear that they're next. But, more importantly, those at the upper end of the performance spectrum, the champions, feel heartened that unsatisfactory performance doesn't go unpunished.

Take action

When you see a good opportunity, the worst thing you can do is sit on your hands and think about it. If it's a good opportunity, just go out there and actually do it. With focus and strong action, anything can be completed.

If it's a good opportunity, just go out there and actually do it. With focus and strong action, anything can be completed.

My view is that right now, the economy is still post-GFC. Certain sectors like mining and potentially the Internet are going strong. This is the best time to be doing deals because valuations are at rock bottom.

Future trends

I'm bullish on the Internet because that's pretty much all I do these days. Where I think there is going to be opportunities is around transactions; whether it's digital currency or just typical, normal currency, and being able to put together a transactional model around that, using efficiencies and leveraging efficiencies of the Internet.

The economics have changed; SAS (software as a service) and online accounting systems are very much the way of the future. People think SMS is old, and it *is* old compared to some other technologies, but there are more and more SMSs being sent on a daily basis. From doctor's surgeries to business owners to some big corporates, they all use SMS as a way to contact and communicate with their customers.

We're starting to develop applications for smart phones. My view is whether it's SMS, iPhone or Android; it's getting to the customer and communicating with them across whatever platform they want. It's being agnostic with regards to what technology you use, just being more customer-focused and saying, "What does this group of customers want, and how do they want it?" and providing it.

> It's being agnostic with regards to what technology
> you use, just being more customer-focused and
> saying, "What does this group of customers want?

Survey Monkey

You can get a quick survey up and running on Survey Monkey in less than 10 minutes. Shoot an email out to your top 50, top 100 customers, and let the customer tell you what they want. I've worked out that the smartest people that we can get feedback from are our customers because they're the ones that are actually buying our product and service. I can spend as many days, weeks or years thinking about it, but ultimately, I really know nothing. The customer knows everything. So from that perspective, ask the customer and give them exactly what they want.

Case study: MailingLists.com.au

Before MailingLists.com.au, if you wanted a mailing list–say you wanted to target coffee shops in Melbourne or you wanted pharmacies in Sydney–you'd have to go to a list broker. It would take a couple of days to turn it around, and they typically charge a minimum fee of $500 or $1000, then they charge you a per record fee.

Why do you need to speak to someone in relation to doing all this? Why can't you just do it online? Why can't I select what state, what industry, what category, click a few buttons, put in my credit card and get an Excel spreadsheet which I can import into virtually any type of CRM platform to do an email-out, or a postal mail-out, or a fax out and just give the control to the customer?

We have orders coming through at 3am or 4am–I don't know what those business owners are doing. Maybe they can't sleep and they think, How do I grow my company? Let me get onto Mailing Lists and do a marketing campaign to try to generate more leads and more customers. It's one of those things you couldn't typically do with a broker and because it's a completely self-service, automatic platform, the cost of the list is significantly less than a traditional broker.

From that perspective, that's just a beautiful example of how you can take an existing old-economy business model, add an Internet layer to it, remove all of the inefficiencies, and provide a much better service at a much better price, 24/7 to customers.

Cydney's Social Wealth Actions Steps:

1. Review your freedom team. Do you have the right people in the right seats on the right bus?
2. How robust is your business model, niche and industry? Take stock of the current economy, the future and evaluate your prospects accordingly.
3. Perform due diligence on your own company. Then consider if acquisitions would make sense to accelerate your business growth. In today's economy, there are plenty of existing web-based businesses that can be acquired as well as offline businesses for sale.
4. Do a review on your own workload and how you spend your time. Are you really working where you should be in your organization or is it time to do some delegating, or move to another role?
5. Add the use of mailing lists to your marketing mix if appropriate. Keep in mind that physical mailings can be more effective than emails as inboxes become increasingly overcrowded.

CHAPTER 23

REPLACE YOURSELF WITH OUTSOURCING

John Jonas

Founder, Replace Myself and
OnlineJobs.ph

John has been making a full-time living online since 2004. He is responsible for helping thousands or entrepreneurs succeed in their online businesses by teaching them how to properly outsource their work. He created ReplaceMyself.com, OnlineJobs. ph and TrackLabor.com to help entrepreneurs implement everything they need by outsourcing all the work. While making a full-time living he rarely works full time, at least not since he was forced to replace himself in his business with full-time Filipino workers. John has made millions of dollars online directly from work that his Filipino workers have done for him and now teaches others exactly how to do the same thing.

From crisis comes clarity

A little over three years ago, my wife was seven months pregnant with our third child. We had two other kids at the time, and we went into the doctor's office, and he comes in and says to my wife, "You have pre-eclampsia, and if you don't go on strict bed rest for the next three to five weeks, you're going to go into seizures and die, and you're going to lose this baby."

At the time, I was running my own business, working full time, and I just remember thinking, "What am I going to do? How am I going to deal with this? Because I'm not about to lose a baby over money."

So I sent an e-mail to two of my guys in the Philippines. I said to them, "Your job now has to change. Here's my situation: I can't work. I need you to do everything that I'm currently doing in my business, take care of my AdWords account and my websites and blog, customer support, our software and bugs, our forums and comments, all the marketing we're doing, articles and videos." For the next three weeks, I worked one hour. My wife had the baby, and for the next two months, I worked one hour a week because I had replaced myself in my business with these other people.

It was such an amazing experience. I never knew how good these people were. Before this, I had been totally under-utilizing them. I had no idea how good they were and what they could do for me.

Another thing I learned was this is how you live lifestyle. The reason I got into the Internet business in the first place was so I could work less. Now I knew this is how you do this.

Just so you are aware of what happened, these were not new people doing this for me. I had these guys working for me for about 18 months, so I had trained them. I hadn't pulled them off the street and all of a sudden they're running my business for me.

The system works!

We made about $800,000 during those three months; I had set the business up to go pretty well and it was going to make money regardless. But the point is that my business didn't fall apart when I wasn't there because there were other people there doing the work. Also, they weren't Harvard MBAs. These guys were making about $250 US per month for full-time work, a business expense, so it's tax-deductible. I'm not paying insurance, I'm not paying their taxes, I don't have an office so I don't pay utilities or anything like that. After tax savings, this $250 is really like $180 a month that I'm paying for full-time work, and these guys are running my business for me.

I have a goal of getting a million people overseas jobs. That's one of the reasons I'm doing this. The second reason is because I love watching entrepreneurs succeed. This outsourcing is not sending an entire division of the company overseas and costing thousands of American jobs. This is about you hiring an individual person to do your work for you, the work that you are currently doing, so that you can work less.

Here's the general idea of how you're going to do this: you're going to hire a single person. You're going to hire them full-time and you're going to teach them everything you know about your business, so that over time, they can start running your business for you. It's not going to happen overnight. You're going to have to train them. But they'll do amazing things for you.

I'm not talking about hiring a contract worker here, a freelancer who's going to do a project and then you're done with them. The problem with that is it's not automation. The problem is that once you're done with that person, you never benefit from their knowledge again. You also never benefit from any effort you put into the relationship with that person. It's gone permanently and the next time you want to get something done, you have to go out and find another person to do it. It's really not a good way to run a business.

One of the problems with doing business on the Internet is it's a technical business. I graduated from college in computer science and when I think about all the things I have to do in my business, it scares me. It should really just come down to you communicating with someone else who knows how to do these things and can do it very well, and very cheaply, where all you have to do is just tell them what you want.

The main problem I find that people have, and it's a problem I had, which is knowing what's possible with outsourcing. Traditional outsourcing has all these problems associated with it: communication problems, poor work and late deliverables, and it can be very different than that. I'm going to show you how to make it very different.

Let's talk about the business that I started when it was time for me to start working again, because I had to have something to do. You should be implementing everything you know; I was going to be the CEO of the business.

Everything you know–all the e-books you've bought, the DVD courses, the membership sites you've bought, the seminars you've attended–you should be implementing all these things. You just shouldn't be the one doing the work.

I found and bought the domain. Then I recorded myself talking for 35 minutes about the business; the goals of the business, the direction, why we're doing it, how we're going to accomplish the goals and the steps that we need to take to get it there. I talked my way through the whole thing, and then I sent it to one of my guys in the Philippines; I sent the domain and I sent the audio.

The point isn't that he did everything perfectly the first time; he didn't. The point is that I didn't do the work and the work got done. I'm being the CEO of the business, where I can concentrate on the most important things and he's doing the work for it. That business in the first month made me about $200. Within three months, about $1,000 a month. Within six months, $3,000 to $5,000 a month, and within a year, it's making $10,000 to $15,000 a month, and I didn't do anything for it.

The point isn't that he did everything perfectly the first time; he didn't. The point is that I didn't do the work and the work got done.

Biggest outsourcing secrets

Daily email: I require all of my people to send me an email every single day and I have them answer three things:

1. What did you do today?
2. What problems did you run into?
3. What can I do to help you?

It holds them accountable for what they're doing. Even if they didn't accomplish or finish anything, I still want this email. If they run into a problem, I want to know about it.

Difficult first task when hiring: I was hiring people and they would disappear. So I started giving this difficult first task to weed people out. I wanted to know who was going to stick around and who wasn't.

Offer a low starting wage, then raise the wage quickly. Give bonuses for good work.

Network: Once you've hired someone and you're ready to hire someone else, ask them who they know who you can hire.

Let people figure stuff out. In the beginning, you have to train them, but as you've trained them more, you can start stepping away from your business.

Use Jing: Jing is a screen capture and screen recording software. This is how I run my business. This is how I give feedback to people.

Give them access to your software, to your hosting account, to membership sites, to anything you can. The more you can give them access to, the easier your life becomes.

Retain customs: The first email I ever got from someone said, "Dear Sir." It was the first time in my life that I'd been called, "Sir." I just recommend you respect their customs.

Give them software and eBooks.

Share someone: I don't recommend you hire someone part-time. If you don't feel like you have enough money or enough to do to hire someone full-time, find another employer, hire someone full-time and split their time with that other employer.

Document what you teach them. Be the expert.

Regardless of what you have to do, just go hire someone. This will change your life, this will change the way you think about your business, it'll change the way you run your business. It will change the way you succeed in your business because now you have someone else doing your work for you.

Regardless of what you have to do, just go hire someone. This will change your life.

Currently, the best place to find someone online is at OnlineJobs.ph. I own OnlineJobs.ph, and you can take it for what it's worth when I say it's the best. Also, I have all these trainings I have done for my people over the years and I've saved them all. So I put them together into a system that you can get access to so you don't have to do the training for the people that you hire.

It's a monthly program. The first month is designed for you, the business owner, to get you going quickly, to hire someone quickly without the mistakes. Every month after that is not for you anymore, it's for them. I've tried to make this as easy as possible, so you can hire people with little work on your part. This can be the combination of my knowledge plus your knowledge. If you're an expert on something, great , give them my training so that you don't have to teach them every single little detail and then give them your expert knowledge. If you're not an expert at these things, great, give them my training and get them implementing.

John Jonas has generously gifted a bonus report, *How To Outsource Your Business To The Philippines For As Little As $2.50/Hour!* It's yours for

free. Simply visit www.MillionairesAcademy.com/John_Jonas to download your copy!

Cydney's Social Wealth Actions Steps:

1. By now, some of your systems should be fairly automated. Consider hiring some contractors from a country such as the Philippines to start taking over the work of your other team members.
2. In the meantime, promote your core team to revenue-producing activities.
3. Start creating a training video library of all your business systems and processes. Store them in an online wiki or library account, such as dropbox.com or box.net.
4. You may also prefer to use a more sophisticated project management system such as Teamwork, Backpack or Basecamp. The goal is to train your team once and then be set up to train future contractors automatically.
5. Start out with one contractor first and when they are trained, organized and productive, you can find plenty of resource providers through Millionaires Academy, Onlinejobs.ph or the other agencies listed on our site and in this book.

CHAPTER 24

LAY THE FOUNDATIONS FOR WEALTH

Silva Mirzoian

Founder and CEO, Jump-Start Your Life

Silva Mirzoian is the author of the book Jump-Start Your Life®, as well as the producer and CEO of Passions & Dreams For Success Institute. She was named "Dream Weaver" by Entrepreneur Magazine for her unique ability to weave together the past and present to develop a perfect (and wealthy) lifestyle for women!

There is nothing conventional about Silva. She has defied the odds by not just living, but thriving. Married at 19 for all the wrong reasons, Silva divorced only a year later and was considered an outcast in her Armenian community. Her survival mode kicked in and she decided to take off for a year to travel the world, finally settling in the United States. She embarked on securing her financial independence after having walked away from a mentally, physically and verbally abusive marriage with no money or job. Not wanting to run back to the security of her parents, she decided to launch her entrepreneurial dreams through real estate with the one unused credit card from her single days. Before she reached the age of 30, she had created a net worth of $1,000,000 and went on to launch her own real estate sales/design and construction company, followed by a lifestyle design company. All brought opportunities to work with celebrities and travel the world.

When money isn't enough

While I was creating my success in the real estate business back in the '90s, I was living the jet set lifestyle, traveling around the world and spending the summers in the South of France on a yacht going from one island to the other in the Mediterranean Sea. Then, one morning as I was enjoying the sensational view from the deck, it suddenly hit me: This is breathtaking, but why do I feel this huge emptiness in my life? Why is there a void? What is all this about? It has to be more than just having the ability to travel and spend money as I please. I need to be sharing this blessing with others, but how and with whom?

I remember feeling guilty for being depressed in a magical setting and not knowing what to do. I thought to myself, I have survived three near-death experiences—two major car crashes and being inside a burning house—so there has to be something more for my life. But what?

I thought to myself, I had survived three near-death experiences,
so there has to be something more for my life. But what?

Soon after my return to the US, I was asked by a director of the Salvation Army's homeless shelter to come and speak to one of his groups. I gladly accepted and can honestly tell you that was one of the turning points in my life. I had no idea how sharing my personal success story about starting over in another country with no firm resources or guarantees, walking away from an abusive marriage and making it on my own would inspire them.

There I was, standing in front of them, saying, "Hey! I know how you feel right now. I had to sleep on my brother's couch when I left my own home, but look at me. I'm really not much different than you. We've all been born with the same tools: mind, body, spirit and social tools. The difference lies in what we do with them. What are you willing to do with yours?"

At the end of the session, one by one, they came to me and said, "Wow! You just inspired me to go back to school, to learn a new skill or just simply stop feeling sorry for myself." How can you put a price tag on that? I had just changed a person's life. That was the magic. That experience encouraged me to set up my non-profit foundation, Passions & Dreams Funding, which guides women and children at risk to connect with possibilities in life and create their own financial independence, just as I did.

During that time, I was still involved in running my real estate company, but I soon discovered that I was just as passionate about transforming lives as developing properties. That realization launched my lifestyle development and publishing companies, where I became a best-selling author and speaker all over the world.

Moving your business online

When I first started my businesses, I was not very tech-savvy; most of my client generation and growth of business was based on in-person contact, brochures or direct marketing media. As technology improved and computers became more user-friendly, it was obvious that if you were not visible on the internet, then your business was going to become obsolete. That's when I transferred my business online and, let me tell you, moving your business online opens up a whole new world, as you no longer operate from one location. You have an online presence and people from all across the world are able to learn about and have access to you. It's phenomenal and fantastic! Not to mention that it is so cost-effective. When you consider advertising and the big money you used to spend in print media, online marketing is *the* tool for going global.

To be successful in doing business online, you must establish yourself in the public arena by connecting yourself and your business to like-minded entrepreneurs. But before you can even think about establishing your business, you must first be specific about your business, its intention, your market and your product(s). Once you do, just focus on that. Focus, focus, focus and make it better and different than any other person or product out there. It may take some time to catch on, but the key is to make a difference in a specific area and stand out from the rest.

When I first started, I didn't really know much about websites. I thought it was just a replacement of printed brochures... Wrong! Your website has to grab the attention of your visitor and sell/deliver a service or product that is needed. People from around the world, in all different time zones, will be visiting you, so your website has to do the selling work for you *at all times*.

Once I learned that secret, I quickly made a switch from generic pages about myself and my product. I built a stronger client base by networking, tagging, creating keywords and subscribing to search engines and I finally have a website that connects with my readers. I know I may not reach every one of them, but that's because not everyone is my target.

Now, in later years, I have become more firm about the direction of my online presence and that is building wealth through real estate, primarily for women. Real estate and property development is my passion; I know it inside and out. Additionally, I have a deep-down desire to empower and educate women and young girls around the world with ways to build their financial independence through real estate. Just remember, you are never too young to learn about how to build your wealth!

People from around the world, in all different tie zones, will be visiting you, so your website has to do the selling work for you at all times.

Challenges starting my online community

When I first started, I had to understand how the system worked and make friends with it. That was no easy challenge. There are a lot of people out there who profess to be the best web developer or marketing person in the business, but beware! I have, like many other new entrepreneurs, spent hundreds, if not thousands, of dollars with such people. The best advice I can offer is to ask for recommendations from friends and colleagues.

Nowadays, you don't even need to have an extensive website to showcase your services or products. You can simply start a website or blog within a few short hours. It's so easy! Facebook and Google play a big role in getting the word out about you and your business. I have found that one of the best ways to establish presence and expand your community is through educational or training videos on YouTube. Videos help build a connection with your community and, for me, it seems to have a greater impact.

Recently, I launched my BlogTalk radio show as a way to deliver my training message and establish my expert status for my business. I have learned that to be the fastest way to deliver traffic to your website. My show began in July 2011 and the number of listeners has already increased to over 2,200 people in a 3-month period, while my mailing database has grown to over 5,000.

My best advice when it comes to increasing your online community is to set the procedures correctly up front. If that means bringing in a virtual assistant or hiring your tech-savvy nephew or next-door neighbor, do so. It will be worth it.

Communicating with my clients

No one likes to get an impersonal e-mail or be bombarded with newsletters every other day. It's important that you make your message focused and purpose oriented. When I started to create my new programs, "Women, Wealth & Beyond" and "The Power of Femininity" Retreat, I created a focus group to find out what was important for women and what is missing in today's market. The findings then turned into my product development projects. With that, I began preparing a series of presentations, e-books and interviews with experts in various fields who can better empower today's woman to reach her potential: personally and financially.

The main means of contact with my clients is via Constant Contact e-zines, Facebook and weekly event update newsletters. Communication with your clients is essential; just be aware of the ways and frequency in which you are doing so.

Bigger is not always better

If you have, say, 500 core people who are committed to what you're doing, you can then begin to prepare upscale products and services or you can joint venture with others who offer the things that are lacking within your business niche. First, work on creating quality products and before you know it, you will see your client base grow.

Accelerated wealth secrets:

- Concentrate on building your unique business.
- Strive to make it bigger, better and different.
- Surround yourself with like-minded individuals.
- Reach out to a mentor.
- Invest in your marketing plan wisely.
- Focus on being the best at what you do.

During Donald Trump's financial crisis, he said he was in that situation because he "took his eyes off the ball." What you focus on multiplies, so if wealth is what you are seeking, focus on that. As I've always said, "When I leave this world I want to be totally spent: money, mind and body. I want to exhaust myself because I want to do all the things that I love to do. You have to have the passion for what you're doing! You need to have a purpose!" Wealth is everyone's birthright and there's no better time than now to start building your own!

> When I leave this world I want to be
> totally spent: money, mind and body.

Cydney's Social Wealth Actions Steps:

1. Review your website. Is it selling for you 24/7? Is it selling for you at all?
2. Reach out to likeminded entrepreneurs and organize some mutually beneficial joint venture campaigns.
3. Consider starting a 'blogtalkradio' show or podcast. This can be worth doing if you are already recording videos regularly and can use the same audio.
4. Work on developing a high-quality relationship with the people on your mailing list. Bigger is not always better.
5. Review your product and service offer. You may find that you could, in fact, be offering a much higher priced, higher value package to your list once you've established trust and rapport.

CHAPTER 25

MANAGE YOUR EXPOSURE

Jeanette Jifkins

Founder and CEO, Law for Your Website

Born and raised in Queensland, Australia, Jeanette was a persistent high achiever academically and in competitive sports. She competed in swimming at a national level in Australia, Japan and England. She spent a year in Japan at age 15, then worked two years in the United Kingdom after her schooling, returning to Australia to complete her legal studies. Jeanette completed a Bachelor of Laws, a Master of Laws and graduate diploma in legal practice at the Queensland University of Technology. After more than 13 years of practice, Jeanette turned her energy and persistence toward finding solutions for the limited access to affordable legal services available to small business. Drawing on her experience with commercial transactions with values up to $74 million, Jeanette has created the resources available on her website, www.LawForYourWebsite.com

---

Know your legal obligations online

The Internet has expanded the opportunities to have an exciting marketplace, but you need to be aware of who your customers are. I got interested in "who's looking after the legal side of things." When I speak to my colleagues in the profession, many of them don't know what things like LinkedIn are. They've never used Skype. They're not aware of the extent of resources that are available for business online. I saw that as a gap in the market.

I've developed a membership website which allows people to go through a program to familiarize themselves with the particular legal issues unique to websites. Weekly they learn more or they can access all the information a year in advance. The idea is to give them the tools and resources to check things right away. My objective is to create easy, do-it-yourself instructions. You don't have to find a lawyer at first or if you do have a lawyer, you'll know what questions to ask. It's an education process, and a lot of people don't realize they need it until they get into trouble. If you want to build a business online and make money, you've got to understand where your risks are.

It's an education process, and a lot of people don't realize they need it until they get into trouble.

The seven legal essentials for online business

My specialty is identifying what's absolutely essential and how to use that to a budget. The most important thing if you're going to do business is to make money. Know how you're making money before you do anything else.

You can access these "Seven Legal Essentials" from www.LawForYourWebsite. com. What I've done here is summarize and put in some useful advice:

1. Get a domain name that doesn't tread on anybody else's toes and get you into trouble.
2. Find out what you can and can't do with your content, copyright, trademarks and intellectual property; learn about not copying other people's stuff and protecting your own.
3. Consumer protection issues. When you're marketing online, there are things you can and can't say in advertising and things you shouldn't say about your products and services.
4. How to protect your business when people are commenting on your website. A lot of businesses are asking their customers to provide feedback and comments. Make sure what other people put on your website fits within your rules and doesn't get you into trouble.

5.   Privacy. Your privacy obligations are important; they're changing and increasing all the time. You need a policy and procedures in place to support your privacy obligations.

6.   How to search an Australian trademark. When you create your URL, don't use someone else's registered trademark. In the membership area there are videos to show you how to check different trademark registers around the world.

7.   Make your websites accessible to people with disabilities. If your website is accessible, you're potentially expanding your market.

Trademarks and copyrights

Where is the value in my brand? Is the brand going to be at risk as soon as I put it out there? Branding is very important. If your business is online and is going to have a targeted market, look at your competitors and whether the value is in the brand or the products.

If the value is in the products, then do something about protecting your brand, but don't prioritize spending a lot of money getting it trademarked before you start making an income. When you first start promoting, the brand is not necessarily the first thing that identifies what you're doing. People are keyword searching on what they want, not necessarily on a brand.

Put the world on notice that you intend to take action to protect your brand by putting a little capital TM after it. In branded trademarks you usually see an R in a circle after them; that means it's registered. If you don't have your trademark registered, it is important to have records that show; "This is how I came up with the trademark. This is when I started trading under this mark." It means you save money and it doesn't lock you into a brand if you haven't spent a lot of money registering it.

Copyright vs. trademark

Copyright is over creative works, but bigger creative works. You can't copyright something that is very short. Generally speaking, you can't copyright a title, for example, the title of a book or the title of a movie. Copyright is automatically protected; you don't have to register it anywhere. There are some registers around the world, like in the EU and the United States. For trademark protection you do need to register, and there are trademark registers around the world.

You can trademark something short, such as Nike's "Just do it." "Just do it" is a trademark of Nike, but is too short to get copyright protection. However, Nike's tick is both a trademark and capable of protection by copyright because it's artistic.

It's important to pick the government-endorsed trademark registry. There are a lot of sham registries. Be aware of the difference between trademarks and copyright, how you use them and the requirements behind protecting them.

Put the world on notice that you intend to take action to protect your brand by putting a little capital TM after it.

Protecting brand and intellectual property

Look at the value in everything you do. Assess what time and money you put into protection, based on the income you're making from everything you've developed. There are easy things you can do. If you don't want to have to go to court and your material is predominantly online, you can now register it through different online registers. Do a search online for "registering copyright in the United States" and you will find the U.S. official register for copyright. Using the U.S. one as an example, it gives an effective date stamp and authenticity to what you've created. It says you're the owner. Copyright is protected automatically upon creation, but this gives you a less expensive avenue to enforce protection of your copyright without necessarily having to go to court.

There isn't a copyright register in Australia. If you want information about copyright, some of the best site is the official government resource, the Copyright Council. There is also artslaw.com.au for creative arts. If you don't understand it all, visit my website where I've simplified a lot of the copyright issues.

Using music online

You can get a license from organizations such as APRA and AMCOS. If you search "music license" or "license music," you'll find organizations to which you can pay an annual license fee. That will allow you to use certain music for broadcasting purposes. Go into the terms and conditions of these websites and find out what you can and can't do with the music you download. To put music on your website, the best thing is to link to it. Then you're not creating an infringement, just sending people somewhere else to show the same thing. Beware not to encourage illegal downloading.

Want background music? There is public domain music and license-free music available to download all over the Internet that musicians from around the world are creating and putting out there for you to use.

Protect your client relationships

Your clients can be anywhere in the world. Have terms and conditions on your website or terms of use. They are given different labels around the world. If you've got terms, then you're telling visitors to your website, "This is how I do business. These are the rules around what I'm doing. If you have any issue with me, these are the ways to contact me."

If you're going to have a membership website, have your terms of membership up to date. If you're taking email addresses and contact details, have your privacy terms up to date. Have an ability for people to provide feedback. Let people know if they're going to have a dispute with you and want to pursue it, where to go to do that. In this way, you ensure that it is easier and more cost effective for you to defend any claims that may be made against you.

Mailing list essentials

The World Wide Web is a little bit like the "Wild Wild West." There's a whole lot going on out there, but it's not completely without laws and law enforcement.

There are companies able to register your domain names, companies able to provide Internet services and companies that can provide email services. These companies are licensed by ICANN, which is the Internet Corporation for Assigned Names and Numbers. The rules they have to comply with are not to promote spam and to protect personal information.

The basics for sending out emails that are not spam are:

1. You must have the recipients' permission.
2. Your list must understand what kind of material they'll be receiving.
3. You must have an unsubscribe facility on all of your emails.
4. You must provide identification of a real business, either a postal or street address, depending on where you are in the world.

AWeber is the auto-responder program that I use. It's software where I can put details in and emails will go out either on a timed basis or when I say. One of AWeber's requirements is that your subject lines on your emails don't contain words or expressions that are likely to be considered spam. If enough of my emails end up in spam filters, then AWeber is likely to suspend my account. If you're running a business, you don't want your email service provider to suddenly stop sending out your emails; that would be a disaster. It can mean a delay in your business for weeks to persuade your email service provider that you weren't sending out spam, it was a simple mistake, but they should eventually give you your privileges back. The more negative feedback your accounts get, the more likely your Internet or email service providers are going to cut off your business.

One of the first things I say to everybody is have a privacy policy and basic terms of use. You've got to start there and then depending on what your products and services are there are different terms and conditions that you can add into that information as you grow.

Google may not be a government, but it's one of the largest search engines in the world and if you are not going to comply with their rules, you're going to lose your rankings. That means losing business. One of those fundamental requirements is having a privacy policy.

My objective now is to provide legal services in a cost-effective and accessible way. I'm really looking at the opportunity to create a virtual law firm, one where we don't have to have the office space and we can have people available 24/7 if need be.

Cydney's Social Wealth Actions Steps:

1. Should your logos and taglines be trademarked? Do you need to take extra care to register and copyright protect your copy?
2. Is your domain URL legal and not infringing on another company's trademark or brand?
3. Are your privacy policy, terms and conditions and competition terms all compliant with the law?
4. Is your copy compliant with Google's terms and conditions? This is especially important if you advertise with Google, but even if you don't, your website won't rank well with them if you aren't following their "rules."

Are your emailing practices compliant with the anti-spam legislation? For these and other issues please visit Jeanette's site LawForYourWebsite.com.au or, for US residents, AutoWebLaw.com.

CHAPTER 26

A NOTABLE JOURNEY OF OPPORTUNITIES

Aggie Kobrin

CEO, CEC Global Events and Off Hollywood Media

Aggie Kobrin is an entrepreneur and consummate networker with more than ten years of experience in the conference and event management industry and many more spent developing business ventures. Whether she's designing or coordinating an event, consulting to or distributing an independent film, finding talent or creating a new business enterprise, her business philosophy has always been to act with integrity and honesty. A regular on TV and radio and a contributing author to several books, her clients and network include several women's groups and organizations that range from Fortune 500 companies to not-for-profit groups. She has degrees in Psychology and Business Administration from York University in Toronto, Canada.

Providing the network environment

When I started organizing conferences in Southern California in 2004 and 2005, we had upwards of 500 people in attendance. I certainly didn't expect anywhere near those numbers. I quickly recognized that women were hungry to meet other like-minded women and network. In time I became involved with more eminent women's organizations. It was a time when women wanted to meet other like-minded women to learn from and to form alliances.

There's a lot more opportunity now, as women are getting more and more into the entrepreneurial world and realizing its benefits. But at that time there weren't many such opportunities and that's what I was offering.

Then I became involved with the eWomenNetwork, which is a very large and successful women's organization with more than 25,000 members. I was the Regional Manager for Southern California for four years. That launched me deeper into the world of women entrepreneurs. I met some amazing people and became involved in a variety of very exciting projects, including independent filmmaking and distribution. Following the incredible success of *The Secret*, I became involved in several films and was able to get them worldwide distribution. I was amazed at the number of excellent films that were being developed by talented people that don't find an outlet. It was a real waste of talent. We then launched Off Hollywood Media, a film distribution venture. We planned to create a new and exciting way to give the public access to these excellent independent films as well as some television projects that were presented to us. *The Secret* was a tremendous phenomenon that demonstrated the role that Internet marketing can play in distributing independent film. In fact, I believe the film is still selling in certain parts of the world where it didn't get exposure until recently.

The Women Speakers Association

This is an idea whose time has come. Liora Mendeloff saw a gap, a niche. She convinced Gail Watson and I to join her in this very exciting and unique venture. The association is growing through word of mouth and emails, and lots of great blogs. The organization has exceeded its target. In three months, it had attracted a core council group of fifty women who are the "who's who" in the world of speakers, facilitators and coaches. Through their involvement it now has more than 1,000 members worldwide. How did we do it? The fifty core members went out to their databases and followers and the women flocked to the concept. It really resonated with them because, like us, they believed this was an association that could bring about some much needed change in the industry. This was reinforced for me when I recently attended a large speakers association meeting and noted, sadly, that there wasn't one single woman on the stage.

When we first started, we sent invitations through social media platforms like Facebook and called our extensive networks. We told them that they needed to be a part of this. Then we started to hear from people we didn't call, asking why we didn't call them.

Facebook, Twitter and LinkedIn are just a few of the amazing communication media platforms available to people to grow their businesses. Those of us who have over 1,000 Facebook friends and thousands of contacts on LinkedIn can get the message out in a matter of minutes. But one should never forget the power of the telephone and any face-to-face meeting opportunity. You need to be clear that the message you deliver is authentic and provides value. I believe the WSA is and does.

One should never forget the power of the telephone and any face-to-face meeting opportunity. You need to be clear that the message you deliver is authentic and provides value.

The "Truth Behind the Curtain"

"Truth Behind the Curtain" was a significant and difficult decision for me, and another opportunity to make a difference. I've been witness to many difficult situations for several years in the many industries I work in, whether it's with motivational speakers, independent film or the Internet broadcast industry. While recognizing that there are a lot of growing pains in any emerging industry, I feel that too many people were greedy and unethical and I want to help change that or at least expose it. I've always been a very positive person who sees the world not as it is but as I would like it to be.

A small group of people saw a way to have some influence on an industry that could help bring some much-needed changes to it and to the people it serves. We started with an idea and a talented writer and developed a highly entertaining fictional book designed to make people more aware, more informed and more discerning. We added a social media expert and vastly improved our opportunities for getting the word out. Once again, we need to recognize the power of the Internet–social media and social marketing–and the power of truth in empowering people to alter their direction. I find that when I'm engaged in something of value, I attract the help of people with the right skills to make it work. That's the power of good.

When I'm engaged in something of value, I attract the help of people with the right skills to make it work. That's the power of good.

The age of sharing

As an entrepreneur, I recognized very early that the way to succeed is by harnessing the talents of others. It's not what we know but understanding how others can help us build our business and how we can help one another succeed. Learning the benefits of media and social media and appreciating the skills of people in areas such as search engine optimization, blogging, communicating and other technology-related endeavors is the gateway to business success. You can't do it all yourself, so you work with the best. I find people today much more open to giving and sharing. People are finally acknowledging that there's plenty to go around for all of us.

Our plan with 'The Truth Behind the Curtain" is to build a community and develop some other venues, like an Internet show or a film. Again, there's so much talent available. One just needs to connect with the right people who have good intentions. The objective is to educate people on how to find the right people, avoid the charlatans and gain access to the best tools to help them achieve their personal goals.

I want to be involved in projects that are respectful and genuine. It's heartwarming to see how many people agree and are ready to help in any way they can. When you harness the knowledge, good intentions and energy, it can be life-changing.

Accelerated wealth secret:
Crowdfunding—opportunities for financial support

One of the most difficult aspects of building your business is getting financing. I'm also involved in an exciting new venture that will help people receive seed funding for their projects. Crowdfunding is not new, but is still in its infancy. Our project, FunderThunder, joins about 20 other web-based sources in this exciting new business space. The crowdfunding process is based on a micro transaction model, when a large number of people provide a small monetary donation to raise funds needed to complete a particular project.

Believe it or not, if you have an idea or a project, people are willing to help you for very little in return. The generosity of people is astounding. Thousands of people have been given hundreds of thousands of dollars to fulfill their dreams. I'm very excited about this and happy to lend my help. It's another example of the power of social media and social marketing.

Social marketing is the future

I find social marketing very exciting because it's the culmination of everything I've done and learned in my business. Networking comes easily to me. When I'm at an event my first thoughts are about linking people up who can benefit from knowing each other. My work as an event planner and entrepreneur is effortless and I find it very fulfilling. I'll never stop developing and attending events and building my network. That, supported by the online world of social networking, is truly the best of both worlds.

I find social marketing very exciting because it's the culmination of everything I've done and learned in my business.

This doesn't come naturally to people of my generation, but our children and their children will take it for granted and for them it will be second nature. You have to master this way of working and living. The future is now.

Success tips

There are now seven billion people in the world and there's plenty of room for everyone. They say that you could easily fit everyone into the state of Texas. That translates into a lot of talent, skill and a lot of human energy. We need to take care of each other by being honest and genuine. That's how we will change the energy of the world, and I like associating with people who energize me. The secret to business and life success is to be true to ourselves, keep our word, avoid taking advantage of others and believe in the possibilities.

Cydney's Social Wealth Action Steps:

1. Consider live events for bonding on a deeper level with your network and forming strategic alliances.

2. Join associations that can provide support, connections and credibility.

3. Be wary, as you grow your business and start to venture into the open frontier of new media, that there are a lot of scammers, con-men and sharks who will happily liberate you of your success and profits if you are too trusting.

4. Outside investment and crowdfunding can be a means to provide you with funding to grow your business more quickly. There are plenty of investment monies around, but you will need to present a professional investment memorandum and have viable and predictable growth opportunities for most investor options.

5. Social networking seems to be second nature for many of the younger generation, so consider having some of them on your team.

CHAPTER 27

MOBILE: THE NEXT FRONTIER

Adrian Tatham

CEO, Alacrity Technologies

Adrian Tatham, is the founder and CEO of Alacrity Technologies. He's been specializing in interactive communications for the past ten years after decades of experience in the public and private sectors, both in Australia and internationally. In 1999, Adrian's dedication to addressing the need for real-time interactive business communication led him to create Alacrity Technologies, to develop the core technologies that today underpin the innovative CLEW communications platform. Prior to founding Alacrity, Adrian enjoyed sales and project director positions at multinational IT services companies. He began his career in the Australian Customs Service, working for more than 20 years in areas including investigations, law enforcement and implementing new technology strategies.

Alacrity Technologies won the prestigious industry AIIA 2011 Award for Research and Development for their Closed Loop Environment for Wireless.

Taking marketing to the next level

We've created the first offer, order, fulfillment, pick and pack, dispatch and invoicing system across a mobile phone network, without an app in the phone, for anywhere in the world. It's all done in a matter of seconds at negligible cost to the end user because the amount of data that's being transmitted to the phone is less than 10 kilobytes. It's cheaper than an SMS and eliminates the multiple back and forth.

Alacrity Technologies owns a suite of products based on a patented technology called CLEW (Closed Loop Environment for Wireless), developed to address the need for not just interaction with people using mobile phones, but to wrap some intelligence and security around it. Broadcast tools like SMS are great when it relates to static information, but we wanted to allow people to interact, complete business transactions or get information that was real time, like share trading and reactionary capability. This enables them to get time-critical information as it relates to them and be able to react to that. We designed this tool to be carrier, network and device "agnostic." That way, you aren't reliant on company, to the exclusion of others, to be able to complete this. The application is not resident on the device or on the SIM card. It doesn't matter if users change devices, or how fast the devices get, the process is still the same.

One of the pilots we ran was with the Red Cross Blood Service. We identified that if you are looking for O+ blood in a location and broadcast an SMS to all the blood donors, you create a problem. If you send out 3,000 SMSs, the phone system will crash because of so many people making appointments at once. Then you have disgruntled volunteers and donors, because they turn up to your call for help and find they have to stand around for hours.

The distinction of the CLEW technology is that it's not just a one-way text message. When respondents reply to a message, they have visibility of the appointment book, they can see what times are available and pick one. It's much like booking an airline flight on the web; if the seat is not available, you don't see that seat on the flight. We discovered that we'd actually developed cloud computing for mobile phones by allowing people to respond to information through a cloud into a back-end system.

What it means for business

Organizations need to realize that they can leverage mobile technology at a very low cost. If you employ a call center, operators ask questions and then type in the responses. That all costs money. Our clients were saying, "We employ 5,000 people in our call center and we're trying to reduce costs by sending it to the Philippines or India."

We said, "But if you target the people correctly, on a ubiquitous tool, with time-critical information, you're not annoying prospects or clients because they can come to it when they like. When they do come to that message or that information, they're getting it in real time."

Essentially, this type of mobile technology replaces all that pricey infrastructure and labor by making a data session available, where the recipients complete the responses themselves, as if talking to the call center operator. We took that process and streamlined it. One of our clients has 440,000 members and they can send out an offer on 1,000 golf clubs to all their members, who can see if there are now only 500 left, or 300, or the last one, because it's all in real time.

Organizations need to realize that they can
leverage mobile technology at a very low cost.

Secure order and payment processing

An organization that has members with accounts can process orders through our technology. For example, we send out their offer to you, we authenticate by various means that it's you. We've made you an offer of tickets to the Miss Independence Ball. You've told us that you want two tickets and give us your user ID and password. We don't collect credit card numbers or bank details, because the organization already holds that information. We send your order back to the organization. They push the order through to their validator and processor, which says, "That's correct. Here's her receipt number," which is displayed on your phone. We can follow that up with an e-mail or mailed receipt.

It's highly manageable and secure. It doesn't matter if someone else uses your ID and password; we interrogate the device, we question you and we cross-reference that to the information that's coming out of the organization that's making the offer. If things don't match, there are some challenges that need to be made. It's ideal for people who have a client base, have all their clients' information on file, or retailers who do regular specials to their clients, anyone who has their customer information on file already, or plans to.

Managing resources/Rostering

Here's another example of how the system can be used. The Catholic Education Office had 57 schools in an archdiocese with 1,400 teachers on the substitute teacher list. Every day, a teacher doesn't turn up to one of the schools. This means a senior teacher is calling 1,400 people on the list, spending hours to find a replacement teacher.

Our technology works with the HR system and says, "Give me a list of the ninth grade math teachers that are available." It might be 50 teachers. We send them out a CLEW message and the first teacher to apply gets the job and the other 49 are informed when the job's gone. The database at the school is updated so we know that teacher has a job for the next three days. If a job for a ninth grade math teacher comes up in another school, here's the other 49 teachers that are available. The data gets fed on to the payroll system so that teacher gets paid. The school gets notified that they are on the way. We do it in a minute and a half and we charge them a flat fee, typically around $1.

Any business or organization that has to do a lot of phone calling, like following up on clients or chasing them for overdue payments, can utilize this technology. It can be automated for hardly any cost.

One client has a loyalty program; they email discount vouchers. Then they send out a reminder to say, "You've got a discount voucher at your favorite perfume shop and it expires tomorrow. If you present it within the next 24 hours, you'll get double the discount." Then you can track that response. The diagnostic tools are incredible. You want to be able to measure "Am I just spraying out a whole heap of SMSs or am I actually interacting with these people?"

Accelerated wealth secret:

The goal here is to put your business in front of your customers on their terms. Today, that's mobile technology. Our platform may need a little tailoring, but finding a substitute teacher is the same as finding a train driver, a volunteer firefighter, a blood donor. It's only the business rules and the descriptions that really change. The technology doesn't change, so it's pretty simple to set up.

Ask yourself how you can be leveraging mobile technology in your business. Then don't be surprised when you start making more money with less overhead.

The goal here is to put your business in front of your
customers on their terms. Today, that's mobile technology.

Cydney's Social Wealth Action Steps:

1. Consider adding mobile technology to your marketing mix.
2. Review operations now performed manually in your business and consider if this could be more effectively and much more economically performed by a computerized system.
3. If it fits your business; create a loyalty program or weekly special that you can offer your prospects and existing customers that continuously offers them value and cements your brand in their lives with regular reminders.
4. The longer you resist new technologies, the further you will fall behind. Mobile technology can be easily implemented into your business model to take the place of more cumbersome tools.
5. The secret to building a global brand is creating systems and solutions. Review your customer experience from introduction to execution of repeat sales. Strip back your systems to make the experience as easy and joyful for the customer as possible.

CHAPTER 28

SOCIAL EMPOWERMENT, ULTIMATE LEVERAGE

Cathy Burke

CEO The Hunger Project, Australia

Cathy has been the CEO of The Hunger Project Australia for 14 years. She's spent extensive time in villages across India, Bangladesh and Africa, as well as held a number of senior leadership roles within the organization globally. She's a sought-after speaker on transformational leadership and is a powerful advocate on the role women must play as leaders both in Australia and overseas.

Prior to working at The Hunger Project, Cathy worked in federal politics as a senate campaign manager, lobbyist and policy strategist. Cathy received an award for leadership at the Australian Davos Future Summit in 2007.

Sharing good fortune on a grand scale

I love this question May Oliver poses in her poem "Summer Day:"

Doesn't everything die at last, and too soon?
Tell me, what is it you plan to do
with your one wild and precious life?

In many ways it's at the core of my life and work. What drives me is the power of transformation. We live at a critical time in human history, where our social challenges are compounded by climate challenges, hunger and poverty. At the same time we suffer a collective spiritual ennui, a profound sadness and resignation that has us believe we cannot make a difference.

This time also presents profound opportunities for growth, meaning and connection. What's so incredible about living in such a challenging world is that the more we engage in bringing wholeness and integrity, the more human we become.

What are our lives about, really? Is it to only to be comfortable, consume and die? I don't think so. I'm a girl from Perth. After the birth of my first child I felt differently about the world. I just couldn't imagine what mothers went through giving birth to children they knew would die of hunger. This made me receptive to the mission of The Hunger Project and when one of their volunteers spoke to me about the organization's commitment to end hunger, the boldness and vision of it spoke to my spirit.

After being financial supporters, Steve (my husband) and I were invited on a leadership trip to Ethiopia. This invitation was like "heeding the call," to reference Joseph Campbell. So, for many reasons, I ended up in Ethiopia. One place we drove through was called the Valley of Death. About six or seven years earlier, when that really bad famine happened that catalyzed Live Aid, hundreds of thousands of people were on the march to find food. More than 100,000 people died in this valley. They walked into the valley but didn't have enough strength to walk out and they perished in that place. It was eerie and sobering driving through.

We went into a group of villages in a place you won't find on a map. Our group was led by Lynne Twist. She wrote *The Soul of Money* and she's an amazing woman.

We were met by sick children, hardened women and men lying near their huts, willing themselves to die so as not to be a burden on their community. It was so horrific. I just felt, what am I doing here? It was incredibly confronting. I felt alien to everybody I was with. I was not experiencing the oneness of our shared humanity. I felt just totally adrift.

Lynne was completely present. She was radiating love. She connected with people so authentically. She picked up a baby, chatted to the mother through an interpreter and I just thought, That's amazing.

We went to the tribal chief and Lynne said to him, "We're from The Hunger Project. We're not here to give you aid or food. We're here to be your voice, to take your voice and your community out into the wider world so that hunger ends."

I stood there and I had my black sunglasses on, trying hard to keep it together, tears coming down. It just seemed so inadequate.

And the elder said this thing that was just extraordinary. He looked at us and he said, "We don't want your aid or your food anyway. We haven't had any NGO or government here for the last 20 years and we're not looking for that. If our living and dying means that others don't have to live and die like us because of what you take home, then our lives will be worth it."

We went back to the little hut that we were staying in, everyone upset. There were about 10 of us, some crying. People felt so hopeless. "We had biscuits, milk and blankets in the car and we didn't do anything," some accused.

Lynne said this thing that would change my life: "They said they didn't want it and you would only have given to somehow assuage the horror that you've seen, to trick yourself into thinking that you've made a difference today when you have not. The thing you need to do is to keep your promise to these people and go out into the world and be their voice and have hunger end."

I profoundly understand that we are each other.
At the deepest level, I am you and you are me.

As it turned out The Hunger Project did support that community, but I was not to know that at the time. This interaction was my "road to Damascus" moment. I went to Ethiopia as one person and I came home another. Being part of the global movement to end hunger has been my sacred mission since that time in Ethiopia in 1992. I was a volunteer for a number of years and then went on staff. It's like a silken thread. It's like my commitment. I gave my word and it has shaped who I've become. There's an African proverb: "I build the road and the road builds me." That has been very true for me in this journey.

I now have led more than 20 of those trips and have seen myself transformed into somebody who can be profoundly and authentically with another human being in whatever circumstances. No matter who they are, whether they're a President or Prime Minister, a village woman, goat herder or merchant banker. I profoundly understand that we are each other. At the deepest level, I am you and you are me.

How we design strategies in The Hunger Project is based around that fundamental principle that we are each other and that we actually aren't separate even though it seems that we are. Our organization impacts more than 35 million people around 12 countries in the world. We have 350 staff worldwide because we build and work with volunteer leaders from each country. We've trained nearly 400,000 volunteer leaders. Our absolute fundamental belief is that people are extraordinary. They're creative, capable, productive human beings.

Our role in The Hunger Project is to unlock that entrepreneurialism, creativity, proactivity and leadership so that they get to be the authors of their own lives. Instead of this old "a billion mouths to feed" scenario, the truth is that there are a billion human beings and sparks of light who can be lit to take leadership in their own hunger and poverty, and to play a leading and catalytic role in doing that.

It can look like men and women taking that stand to get their daughters educated. When you've got your daughter working in the field, earning 20 rupees a day, which is maybe 30 cents a day, which is still really critical to feed the family, and you put her into school just on the hope that she'll have a better life than you, that's courage! There isn't even any evidence or proof for it, if you're a village goat herder and you're going to send her and stand up to all the prevailing interests that say to get that girl married and don't waste money on education. To do that is the most incredible act of boldness and vision. There are trillions of acts like that happening every day and every year.

US President Obama and other world leaders are working on the cause with THP, here meeting Sharmi Bai, THP trained elected woman leader in India. Photo: The Hunger Project, © www.thp.org

> There will be things that get in your way. There
> will be stuff that doesn't go how you think it's
> going to. Are you still committed to your goals?

Vision, commitment and action

The centerpiece for all of this is the Vision, Commitment and Action (VCA) workshop. It's awesome, and I've sat in on many of these around the world. In the VCA people create a new vision for their lives, commit to it, plan the action and take it. I think anyone reading this can understand this from a business perspective. A dream is crucial, but making it happen is the proof of the pudding.

In the face of any big vision, obstacles will come up. There will be things that will get in your way. There will be stuff that doesn't go how you think it's going to. Are you still committed to your goals?

The Hunger Project's programs are reaching approximately 35,000,000 people

Image used with permission of The Hunger Project © www.thp.org

This stuff really works. A major international consultancy firm did an independent evaluation of our work in Uganda and found that even when THP was no longer working in a community, each year they got stronger in terms of how many leaders were trained, how much money was lent and saved in the bank and a whole bunch of other indicators, which was fantastic.

I'm talking about the harshest of communities in Ethiopia, Uganda, Mozambique, Benin, Senegal. The consultancy firm found our unique point was that we work to shift the mindset before any money goes in there. We're able to do that because we've got really educated, passionate investors who allow us to do that work where you don't initially see any tangible result.

One of the key differences with us is that we're not a service provider. We don't go in and build and do stuff for people. We go in to unlock their own capacity, then they're the ones running literacy classes and volunteer food banks and doing all the different tasks that in other models you would have paid staff to do for them.

So it's not, "Here's $200,000 and I want a school built and a hospital built, go and deliver services." Our work is transformational and long-lasting. At the beginning it may seem like a lot of people are sitting around talking to each other. But this when ownership happens, when people get it for themselves.

Our role is around the money. We so want it to be about something else, like digging a well or something hands-on. But it really is about our own mindset of scarcity and freeing up the resources that can change the world. Money is just the start of the energy. When you start channeling it, it's your love, your connection, your network, your passion.

Money is just the start of energy. When you start channeling it, it becomes your love, your connection, your network, your passion.

Cydney's Social Wealth Action Steps:

1. The Hunger Project is a brilliant example of social business in its traditional form, connecting community members and utilizing relationships and empowerment training to create real and positive change. How can you put their example to work in your business?

2. Evaluate your own business. Are you comfortable with your ethical standards? Could your business run a social division with the emphasis on community over profit?

3. Create the structure in your business model that allows you to partner with organizations like the Hunger Project. You will find that it is not just good for your soul, team morale and your conscience–it's great for business too!

4. When looking for a cause to align your business with, choose wisely. Are the organizations you're considering particularly productive and effective? Do they maximize investor dollar impact?

5. Narrow your list of causes to align with to the top three and choose based on the criteria mentioned in step one, as well as how synergistic the fit is with your own business.

EPILOGUE

When I studied marketing many years ago, we learned that from the time of industrialization to the 1920s, businesses operated mainly on the "Production Concept." Focus was on creating better products ("building a better mousetrap"). In the 1930s, as the market became more sophisticated, many companies found themselves competing against others with similar products, so they adapted to the "Sales Concept." The focus shifted to advertising and selling. Eventually, with market saturation, the "Marketing Concept" evolved and around the 1950s, forward-thinking companies started analyzing the market and customer wants and needs before they developed the products or came up with a sales campaign.

Many companies still operate from a product perspective, and many more from the sales concept. Even though the marketing concept was still quite revolutionary back in the 1980s when I first saw it applied at the management level in businesses, it still seems like brilliance to a lot of business owners when you tell them to find out what their customers want and need before they create the products. But with the Internet at most shoppers' fingertips, everything is changing. For most products, there are a multitude of choices. It also doesn't matter what suburb or even what country the items are for sale in, we can find them in seconds. It might not even come down to price. Now customers are evaluating on "trustworthiness factors" such as reputation, website quality, guarantees, customer feedback, SEO ranking, social media presence and peer referral.

Now, thanks to social media and online forums, the customers have public discussion platforms and plenty to say about what they will buy, have bought and where and how. According to Iggy Pintado, "we're moving from a *transactional* economy to a *relational* economy. People don't just buy products anymore. So your brand needs to be something that people relate to. It has to be accessible and engaging. There must be a connection between your prospects and customers and the products and services you're offering that goes beyond the transaction. How do you become connected? What are the key elements? The basics are still there."

"In our connected digital world, relationships can work for you or against you. It's an imperative that you get it right," says Sharon Pearson. "We're not six degrees of separation anymore. We're one degree of separation, and that's on a slow day, and because of that, the immediacy of contact, connection, communication, we have to be on the ball as providers of services. We have not just an obligation anymore to be good at what we do; it's a business imperative. You can't fake it. You can't blitz the marketing and do a shoddy product. You can't hope to make a sale and then pack up and go overnight. It just can't be like that because there's Facebook and YouTube, and there are 1,000 different ways that the world can get its message out on whether they give you the thumbs up or the thumbs down."

Many of the experts in this book have been brave pioneers running businesses on the Internet for nearly 20 years. They say what works is to understand your customers, solve their problems, nurture and build trusting relationships with the community who will then support and grow your business. Dr. Lois Frankel says, "We all need to build strong 360-degree relationships all the time. By that I mean with people who may be senior to you, peers, people who report to you and even outside vendors. You continually build relationships–even with people you think you would never need anything from–because you don't know which one you'll need in the future."

John S. Rhodes says, "Your business is *you*. Play to your talents and strengths. Align with other industry leaders for exponential reach and impact. If you're not true to yourself then you're done, you're sunk. If you don't know who you are, you can't be true to yourself. You want to be the best you that you can possibly be." To build a long-term relationship with an army of loyal fans, who communicate your message by wearing, drinking, carrying, driving, raving about your products and services, it's all about how you communicate your message.

The clarity of your positioning in your market, the communication and warmth of your brand, and the world-of-mouth reputation your customers are spreading about you all come down to your relationship with them. Lois Frankel adds, "What I've learned is that the more you give, the more you get back in return. It's really about a generosity of spirit. When you are going to build your brand, whether it's your personal or business brand, you have to include a generosity of spirit so that people know you're not just in it for the money."

Armand Morin says the secret is to "know your numbers, provide solutions to common problems, align with or become fans of celebrities who already have fanatic pulling power, build lists to keep communicating–they are the key to everything... Affiliate marketing is the greatest form of marketing. If people are willing to market your products and services for you, they're going to spend their money on ads. They're going to send it to their lists and you're going to reach people that you never thought possible through your affiliate network. By building your own affiliate system into your product or service, you can really expand and leverage all of their connections and all of their resources unlike anything else."

Jim and Emily Graham explain: "There are almost 2.1 billion users of the Internet worldwide, and almost half that number on Facebook. It's growing at a rate of 20,000 new users a day and last year, there was just over $165 billion in revenue from the Internet. That was up 14 percent from 2009, even though there was a global slump. It's projected to grow at another 14 percent this year. Where can you have a 14 percent increase in revenue in any type of business where you are relying upon others? When there are 20,000 new users of the Internet coming on every day and they're into Google, Bing, Yahoo, Facebook, these are opportunities because these people want information. If we can find a need and fill it, or find a problem and solve it, or find a want and complete it, we now have a value proposition."

Jennie Armato elaborates: "Imagine if I could cast my marketing net wider than my current reach and directly to my intended market. Imagine if other people would willingly circulate my information for me; they're not making it up, they're simply passing it on. Imagine if I could go from a local business to a global business for virtually free. There are just over 800 million people on social engines every day and it's growing. With Internet coverage globally of over 75 percent, there's a lot of growing still to do. I'm happy with 1 percent, even 0.1 percent of people picking up my stuff and sharing it until it hits the people that are genuinely interested and qualified for what it is I do."

Dr Joanna Martin advises, "If you want to have an incredible life, you need to have an incredible community. Elements to a great community are your peers and your network. I think part of your millionaire formula has to be hanging out with the right people. Then I think the second component is having the right mentors and advisers. I hope that if my mission for an extraordinary life can inspire others to live an extraordinary life as well, then I think that's a life well served. That's what I really want to do: inspire people to step up and live their extraordinary life."

Finally, I remind you that your reputation on the Internet is now more valuable than your brand. I invite you to use the strategies in this book. Go out and stake a claim on your virtual goldmine. Deliver value, solve problems, create beneficial relationships and your own extraordinary life.

ABOUT THE AUTHOR

Cydney O'Sullivan

CEO, Millionaires Academy &
Innovation Publishing

Cydney O'Sullivan shares her time between two teenagers, consulting, and travelling to international conferences. Although she calls Sydney, Australia home, she was born in the USA and raised in a family of entrepreneurs in British Hong Kong. Following her passion, she has been fortunate enough to own shareholdings in businesses from seed projects to IPOs for over 30 years.

As a business, real estate and stock market investor she has made millions, literally starting her first business with nothing but drive and enthusiasm. But, with her success, she also made some costly mistakes; the most painful lessons learned from taking advice from so-called "financial experts." This motivated her to rebuild her own wealth and, in the process, become a caring mentor, assisting others toward their own success, helping them to find ethical advisors and thus avoid some of the pitfalls and costs of her own inexperience. She is a proud supporter of micro-economic lending and social business and sees it as a mission to promote the amazing works of The Hunger Project, (www.THP.org), Grameen.org, Kiva.org and other such organizations.

Her business advice has been featured in national newspapers and magazines and in the following books: *Secrets of Inspiring Women Exposed!* and *Secrets of Stock Market Traders Exposed!* by Dale Beaumont, *Wake Up Women, Be Happy, Healthy and Wealthy!* by Ardice Farrow, *Women on Top Against The Odds* by Sally

Healey & Terri Cooper, *The Wonderful Web Women - Gold Book 2011* by Janet Beckers, *Women Igniting Change* by Tania Usher, and *Mumpreneurs Online* by Fiona Lewis.

She has also published *How to Be Wealthy NOW! 108 Fast Cash Solutions*, based on her own experience turning value and service into quick cash. The book was written to help anyone needing cash FAST, it's full of practical ideas for home based enterprises and every day advice for families.

She established **Millionaires Academy™ and Innovation Publishing™** as safe havens where enthusiastic entrepreneurs can find guidance from high integrity, established mentors who are achieving extraordinary results in their areas of expertise. She has aligned with some of the greatest business mentors in the world in order to provide the best advice in a crowded marketplace, and recently launched MillionairesAcademy.com™ to showcase the full tutorials and success strategies outlined in this book in the form of a step-by-step, online marketing training program.

www.MillionairesAcademy.com